Peace in the Process

How Adoption Built
My Faith and My Family

KRISTIN HILL TAYLOR

Beth —
May God bless
your family. He put
you all together in
His way on purpose for
purposes.
— Kristin Taylor
2017

Unless noted scripture taken from the Holy Bible, NEW INTERNATIONAL VERSION®. Copyright © 1973, 1978, 1984 by Biblica, Inc. All rights reserved worldwide. Used by permission.

Scripture quotations from THE MESSAGE will be marked The Message. Copyright © by Eugene H. Peterson 1993, 1994, 1995, 1996, 2000, 2001, 2002. Used by permission of Tyndale House Publishers, Inc.

Cover photograph by Makenzie Lynn Photography

Cover design by Angie Wyatt

ISBN-13: 978-1976215902
ISBN-10: 1976215900

Kristin Hill Taylor shares an inspiring and heartwarming story of how God created her family in a way she never expected. For anyone who has adopted, considered doing so, or knows someone on that journey – this book will encourage you.

—Holley Gerth, best-selling author of "You're Already Amazing"

In "Peace in the Process," Kristin Taylor peels back the veneer from her family's journey through infertility and adoption, uncovering the beautiful truth of God's faithfulness. Thank you, Kristin, for your courage in sharing your inspiring story!

—Randall Goodgame, Slugs & Bugs family music creator

"Peace in the Process" is one woman's unexpected journey toward motherhood, but more than that, it's the story of anyone whose life didn't go according to plan. Kristin Hill Taylor shares a beautiful story of how God made a family – her family – through the beauty of adoption. Reading along, I imagined all of the adoptive families who would be richly blessed by reading these words. Even more, I prayed that this book would fall into the hands of many young women who might be weighing that difficult decision about how to handle an unplanned pregnancy. This book tenderly illustrates how God writes the most beautiful stories out of our deepest heartaches.

—Jennifer Dukes Lee, author of "Love Idol" and "The Happiness Dare"

Whether you are going through infertility or a completely different type of struggle, "Peace in the Process" will be a comfort and an encouragement to you as you face a life that looks completely different than you imagined or expected. Kristin's story resonates with me as someone who also has learned to release my expectations and trust God even with – or maybe especially with – things most important to me, and it encourages me to keep placing my family and our future in the hands of the One who designed us and loves us more than I can imagine.

—Mary Carver, author of "Fast Talk & Faith: A 22-Day Devotional Inspired by Gilmore Girls"

To my family of five, I adore us together and
our story is my greatest testimony of God's faithfulness.

To three brave birth moms, I can never say thank you enough
for choosing life for the babies growing inside of you and then
choosing me to be their momma.

Table of Contents

Introduction

Take delight in the Lord, and he will give you the desires of your heart.

(Psalm 37:4)

I didn't dream of being a mom. I just assumed I would eventually have kids.

A people-pleasing, first-born child, I was a good student who went to college and never changed my major. I worked as a newspaper reporter, just as my print journalism degree would have me do. I married my college boyfriend and we started our life together. I went through life as I assumed lives were supposed to be lived.

And then one day in December 2004, I realized the birth control pills I was taking regularly were preventing God from having His way with my family. Like every stereotypical young, American couple, we decided we were "ready" to have a baby. My husband Greg was already ready and was just waiting – quite patiently, I might add – for me to want a family.

Nearly two years went by and for various reasons we were still childless. Yes, I cried out to God when friends announced pregnancies: "I told you I was ready!"

The waiting made me weary. The medicine that helped me ovulate made me cranky. The whole season put a strain on my marriage.

I just wanted to have a baby.

That was the next step in life.

But it wasn't the next step in my life. I did eventually become a mom, never expecting adoption to be our story. But it's a story I tell over and over again because it's the one that changed me.

Adoption built my faith and gave me a family.

On my journey to motherhood, I learned what the peace that passes all understanding really means and how God really does work together all things for His good. I have a testimony of God's faithfulness – something I wouldn't trade for getting my own way when I thought I knew what was best.

To tell the story of God's faithfulness, I go back to the wilderness, when I didn't see God working. I learned much later the wandering through the hard season of infertility was necessary to prepare me for what God wanted to do.

While telling our story, I did change some names to protect people's privacy, but who they are is woven throughout my family. I also invited some friends to share pieces of their families' adoption stories. They're included throughout my story.

How God Works in the Wait

Rejoice in the Lord always. I will say it again: Rejoice!
Let your gentleness be evident to all.
The Lord is near. Do not be anxious about anything, but in every situation, by prayer
and petition, with thanksgiving, present your requests to God. And the peace of God,
which transcends all understanding, will guard your hearts and your minds in Christ
Jesus.

(Philippians 4:4-7)

For most of my childhood, college years and the early years of marriage, I would have told you peace came when life went as expected and I achieved whatever it was I set out to do. Bad grades, disappointments, and shaken plans devastated me. The only reason I didn't shy away from conflict was because I thought I could somehow restore order through it.

One Sunday after church in December 2004, I told myself and my husband I wanted to stop taking birth control pills so God could have His way in us as we started a family.

Translation: I really thought I was ready to become a mom. If history was any indicator, when I decided I was ready, I'd take all the necessary steps and achieve my goal. Contradictory to my task-focused ways, I really did believe I was trusting God.

But it's hard to trust with a grip as tight as mine was then.

I've never been much of a science-minded person, but I knew something was wrong when I didn't have a menstrual cycle for six months after trashing my birth control pills. I knew I wasn't going to get pregnant if I wasn't ovulating.

With my let's-fix-it mentality, I called the doctor. At the end of the appointment, he prescribed Clomid to help me ovulate. I walked out of the doctor's office with just the tool I needed to get my way. I probably should have been more nervous about taking a fertility drug, but I was already desperate for a solution.

Somehow I was still shocked that this next step in life wasn't that easy. Clomid helped me ovulate for five months, according to many vials of blood work, but it also made me emotional – that's the nice way for saying crazy – and added some stress to my marriage.

Even through the emotions, I was convinced this was all part of trying to become a mom. Between the doctor's appointments and blood draws, I prayed, "God, please help us become pregnant." I uttered those six words over and over again – as friends announced their pregnancies, on the good days when I had hope, and on the hard days where I couldn't figure out why I wasn't getting my way.

The doctor didn't know why I wasn't getting pregnant because all indicators showed I was ovulating regularly. We counted days and planned intercourse, but being meticulous doesn't overpower the Maker of life.

I wanted answers and, thankfully, so did the doctor.

Thirteen months after I decided I was ready to have a baby, my doctor performed exploratory laparoscopy surgery that revealed I had endometriosis, which contributed to blockage in both fallopian tubes. He was able to unblock the left one, but not the right one. Endometriosis happens when cells from the lining of the uterus grow in other areas of the body. This can lead to pain, irregular bleeding, and infertility. Fortunately, I didn't have any physical pain associated with this condition.

While I welcomed the diagnosis, the days before the surgery were scary for me. One afternoon before the outpatient surgery date, my best friend Jaclyn and I sat in my car after we walked – which means we exercised as an excuse to talk – and I cried. And cried. And cried.

Jaclyn held my hand and offered encouragement that could only come because she'd been there. She'd struggled to conceive, then miscarried when she finally got pregnant. That ectopic pregnancy caused her to her lose one of her fallopian tubes. Yet that afternoon in January 2006 she was six months into her pregnancy with her first son.

With my diagnosis came hope – and more Clomid. More Clomid meant more emotions and planned intercourse. Sure, it made me crazy, but it would all be worth it when I could finally pee on a stick and announce my pregnancy ... right?

I continued going to baby showers and for the most part kept myself together. I remember the pep talks I gave myself before going to celebrate people I loved and the new lives they were bringing into this world.

But one baby shower got the best of my emotions. This one was in honor of my friend Corbitt. I really did want to celebrate this new life, especially knowing she and her husband had been down the infertility road. Still I wondered when it would be my turn. I fell apart after the shower in the backyard – with Corbitt by my side. Now that's a good friend – coming into my grief because she understood and bringing hope because God had given her new life, literally.

Unfortunately for me, a few more months of Clomid was not the answer to my prayers, cries, demands, and pleas to become pregnant.

My doctor wasn't satisfied with the lack of a positive pregnancy test either, so in July 2006 he performed a hysterosalpingogram – that's a nutty word that means he ran dye through my tubes to see if they were clear. It was an intense feeling, but that didn't matter once my doctor told me both my tubes were clear.

There was no explanation as to how or why both tubes were clear, but we rejoiced.

I laugh when I think about my doctor offering a high five while I wore a hospital gown and still lay on a metal exam table, but it was such an encouragement to my weary self. I realized at that moment he was in this journey with me.

My doctor reminded me science matters when creating life, but it's really about the Creator of it all. God designed our bodies and can have His way with them. He can unblock tubes and create life despite our human imperfections.

I walked out of the doctor's office with hope more than once – and Lord knows I walked in and out of that office more times than I really cared to. There I was again, so ready to give up, and hope seeped back into my life.

———

I don't wear a watch, but I usually know what time it is. I don't like to be late and actually prefer to be a few minutes early. I live as if I'm the time keeper.

Too often I rush the moment. Sometimes I wait until the last minute because I'm trying to send one more email or finish one more chore and have to hurry everyone along because I have a stubborn streak. And then stress escalates and time seems to speed up while others' movements slow down.

I forget sometimes, but I know the actual Time Keeper.

God's time is perfect. He sees the whole timeline and doesn't make mistakes with the seconds, minutes, days, weeks, months, and years.

"Praise be to the name of God for ever and ever; wisdom and power are his. He changes times and seasons; he deposes kings and raises up others. He gives wisdom to the wise and knowledge to the discerning. He reveals deep and hidden things; he knows what lies in darkness, and light dwells with him. I thank and praise you, God of my ancestors: You have given me wisdom and power, you have made known to me what we asked of you, you have made known to us the dream of the king." (Daniel 2:20-23)

God had my season of infertility in His hands. He was working even when I doubted and wondered and tried to do it all myself. I wish I had known then that working harder isn't always the answer. I would have rested in the promises of God and worshipped more instead of working harder.

I was ready to have a baby. My husband was beyond ready. But God said wait.

Waiting is hard, yet it is something we all do. Every day, many times a day, really.

We wait for lights to turn green. We wait for people to return calls and extend invitations. We wait for the mail to be delivered. We wait for dinner to be ready and bedtime to come. We wait for the next season and the next adventure. We wait for babies to be born, job promotions to come, sickness to pass, people to understand what we meant, the necessary finances to come.

We wait.

Waiting was a theme in God making me a momma. The waiting broke my heart, but I have since learned I didn't approach that season the way God intended. I waited for a positive pregnancy test like I was wasting my time. I didn't draw near to God or seek His truth in the moment.

Years after that wait, I read about Ruth waiting for Boaz to resolve the matter of caring for her and her mother-in-law, Naomi, in the proper way. In *Take Refuge*, a study of Ruth, authors Lara Williams and Katie Orr write about how waiting is active. "Wait" means to "bind," which is interesting to remember while reading Isaiah 40:30-31:

> "Even youths grow tired and weary, and young men stumble and fall; but those who hope in the Lord will renew their strength. They will soar on wings like eagles; they will run and not grow weary, they will walk and not be faint."

What if while waiting to become a momma, I had been binding myself to the Lord?

In *31 Days to Coming Alive*, author Jenn Hand prompted me to think about waiting again. Her words reminded me how waiting is always present and an active part of our faith journey. "… as believers, we are ultimately in the waiting. We are waiting for the fulfillment of the promise of heaven. We are in the here-and-now, created with restless pangs of longing for the promise-yet-not-experienced."[1]

We are sanctified and perfected in the waiting.

The light will turn green. The phone will ring. The invitation will come. Dinner will be marinated and baked. It will be time for rest. Spring always comes. New life abounds. Healing comes. God provides exactly what we need.

I have no doubt spending an eternity with our Creator will be worth the wait, too. Waiting to become a mom taught me about living, embracing the here-and-now, knowing waiting is an active part of life. God works in the wait.

———

All the talk of trying to become pregnant monopolized my life. I had a job. Greg had a job. We had friends. We went on trips. But trying to have a family dominated my thoughts. One day in August 2006, I thought about having a family in a way that didn't involve blood vial, pills that made me crazy, and medical procedures. We heard about a local high school girl who was interested in finding a family to adopt the twins she was carrying.

Here I was, wishing and hoping and pleading and praying and crying out to be pregnant, and God stirred within me a new – albeit slightly crazy – hope. We expressed our interest in adopting the twins through the high school principal, but we never heard anything else about it. Looking back, I realize God was planting a seed. It was the first time I'd ever considered adoption.

---

[1] Hand, Jennifer. 31 Days to Coming Alive. Amazon Digital Services, 2014.

Meanwhile, my doctor referred us to a big-city reproductive endocrinologist in that fall – about 21 months after I stopped taking my birth control pills and declared my readiness to get pregnant.

By this time, we also had learned Greg's contribution to the pregnancy equation wasn't helping our odds. The reproductive endocrinologist talked about the possibilities of pregnancy given the issues in both our bodies and, of course, scheduled more blood work for me.

The most basic explanation is my body doesn't make enough of the right hormones to sustain my eggs, meaning the quality and quantity was low. Along with the endometriosis, the specialist strongly suspected I had poly-cystic ovarian syndrome, a condition that would explain my imbalance of female reproductive hormones. So if I were to get pregnant, I'd have to have hormone supplements, too.

My new doctor helped us connect the dots and eliminate or correct any variables that were standing in our way. While he talked about sperm, eggs, ovulating, implantation, I thought about how perfect conceiving life is. The precise timing necessary to create a baby is more exact than anything we as imperfect people can control. In fact, it's perfect, which is proof enough to me that God creates babies. He aligns all the variables and perfects a process inside our imperfect bodies. That is why I believe every baby has a purpose. Now, granted, babies don't come into perfect situations, but they are here for a reason.

With that said, somebody could argue: Why ever go to a doctor if God is control of conception? I'll tell you: We as humans need hope. God gave these doctors minds to help people like me who want to make sense out of what is – or, in some cases, isn't – going on inside our bodies. Even so, God is most certainly in control of making living miracles.

In the following weeks I grasped for more answers and hope, so I read a book called *Infertility: A Survival Guide for Couples and Those Who Love Them* by Cindy Lewis Dake. What stuck with me was a chapter on boundaries. I don't really remember what Dake said, but I do remember coming away with the desire to set some emotional, financial, and physical boundaries.

Having Type 1 Diabetes, I knew pregnancy was going to be physically hard on me. I would require additional insulin shots and would probably experience more blood sugar ups and downs than I had in normal life. I also knew infertility left me emotionally drained. While talking through all of this with Greg, we realized we needed to create boundaries for ourselves before we went to our follow-up appointment with the specialist in Nashville. And this was it for us: If the doctor recommended in-vitro fertilization, we would stop trying to get pregnant and turn our attention, money, and energy to adoption.

In October 2006, after 22 months of trying, a doctor who knew far more than we did told us our best odds of getting pregnant would come with IVF. We thanked him for the information and headed home. In those two hours in the car, I had more peace than I'd had since I threw away my package of birth control pills.

We had absolutely no idea what throwing ourselves into adoption would mean, but for the first time in my life I was experiencing the peace that passes all understanding. And I had yet to learn about a teenage girl who was just a couple months into her unexpected pregnancy.

In Their Words :: Caitlin Dunbar

Waiting seems to have been a theme for Jason and me throughout our marriage. We struggled with infertility for five of our first six years of marriage. We always knew that adoption would be a part of our story, but we weren't sure exactly what that would look like for our family.

When God impressed upon our hearts it was the right time to begin the adoption process, I was so excited and just knew this was going to happen almost overnight. Boy, was I wrong. Adoption is worth it, but it's also hard and messy.

We prayed for direction, filled out so much paperwork, and completed our home study and profile book. After what seemed like FOREVER, we were able to present our profile to birth moms. This was so nerve-racking. Sometimes it seemed like torture as we waited for a phone call stating a birth mom had chosen us. However, we rested in the fact God chose the right baby for our family long ago!

Through adopting, God really began speaking to my heart about waiting. I fought giving up control as hard as I could, hoping to speed up the process myself somehow. I'm the girl that puts an address in the GPS for places I go every day, just to know exactly what time I will arrive. When I finally entrusted God with everything, I was overwhelmed with unexplainable peace. Psalms 62:5-6 says: "Let all that I am wait quietly before God, for my hope is in Him. He alone is my rock and my salvation, my fortress where I will not be shaken."

After seeing countless situations, presenting to many birth moms and hearing several "nos," we finally received our "yes" at the beginning of October 2015. A few weeks later, our daughter was born in Utah. She was definitely worth the wait! It is amazing to look back and see how God orchestrated each and every detail perfectly. She brings so much love, joy, and laughter into our home and is a daily reminder of God's unfailing grace.

Know there is hope in your waiting, whatever the circumstance. Time and time again, we have been reminded of God's completely perfect plan. What I had been looking at through frustrated, confused, and impatient eyes, I now see as ways for God to be glorified in all aspects. We see so many examples of this throughout the Bible. The name of the Lord is made known through the periods of waiting, crazy circumstances, and things far beyond our understanding. Whatever you are waiting for, whether it is big or small, trust in His amazing plan and perfect timing.

Caitlin Dunbar is a wife, mom, and middle school teacher who is passionate about serving Jesus and making Him known through student ministry and adoption. She blogs at BringingHomeDBaby.blogspot.com.

How God Hears Our Desires

For you created my inmost being; you knit me together in my mother's womb. I praise you because I am fearfully and wonderfully made; your works are wonderful, I know that full well. My frame was not hidden from you when I was made in the secret place, when I was woven together in the depths of the earth. Your eyes saw my unformed body; all the days ordained for me were written in your book before one of them came to be.

(Psalm 139:13-16)

I let go of the six words that were always on my mind.

"God, please let us become pregnant" was replaced with questions about what adoption would mean for us. Greg is an attorney so we told some attorney friends about our desire to adopt. We told some doctors, our family, and our friends. I needed an emotional break from making appointments and telling professionals about diabetes, endometriosis, and probable polycystic ovarian syndrome, so we didn't research adoption agencies.

About two months after leaving the specialists' office with peace that certainly surpassed our understanding, God opened a door. On Christmas Eve, my sister Cassie shared what she knew about Mandy, a college freshman who was interested in making an adoption plan, possibly with us.

The hope alone was the best Christmas present ever.

Three days after Cassie spoke hope into our life, I talked with Mandy's mom on the phone. She believed Greg and I were the answer to her prayers and her own daughter's hopes. But her daughter was carrying the baby we discussed, so we had to hand the proverbial ball to her. She needed to sort through plans of her own before getting back to us when she was certain of how she wanted to proceed.

Three weeks really isn't that long, but it sure feels like an eternity while waiting for life-changing news that is in someone else's hands. Yes, another reminder I wasn't in control.

My phone finally rang with an out-of-state area code I recognized during the evening of Wednesday, January 17, 2007, while I was covering a meeting for my job as a newspaper reporter.

————

I left City Hall as quick as I could. Taking notes about the zoning ordinance and the local business' request for a variance was finished for the day. Thankfully, I didn't live far from home and dialed Mandy's number as fast as my fingers would allow as soon as I took a seat at my kitchen table.

Mandy and I quickly realized we were on the same page with wanting to pursue this adoption plan. That was good news enough, but Mandy continued, "And I have a doctor's appointment in the morning. I'll have another ultrasound done, if you want to see the baby."

We wanted to be there – a fact I was confident about even though I hadn't even talked to Greg yet. He came home soon after and we celebrated, briefly. We were thrilled to have such exciting news to share with our small group from church that was already meeting at a home not too far away. It was the kind of news that overshadowed the fact we were late getting there.

I still needed to crank out a Board of Zoning Adjustments article for the next day's paper, but first I needed to call my editor at home.

"I am finishing up my zoning board story, but I won't be in the newsroom in the morning because I'm going to meet the birth mom of our baby," I blurted out.

I'm not even sure my male editor really knew of the infertility season that had plagued my heart, but he was gracious with my last-minute request.

On January 18, 2007, we drove the 258 miles to Bloomington, Indiana, to meet Mandy and see our daughter. In the waiting room at the doctor's office, we had our first conversations with Mandy, who is 5-foot-10 with a sweet face. Her dark hair was mostly straight but seemed to want to flip as it grew longer now that her cancer was in remission.

She could raise the baby growing inside, and truly I have no doubt she'd be a fine mother. But she was just finishing her freshman year of college and thought about pursuing a career in the medical field. I knew then she'd end up helping people. Perhaps that's why she battled and survived Hodgkin's disease, a feat signified by the yellow "LIVESTRONG" bracelet she wore around her wrist.

She's a survivor and she chose life for this baby girl.

At 25 weeks, our baby girl weighed 1 pound 10 ounces. This would be the first of many trips to Bloomington and many lunches with this young, brave woman who was making me a momma.

Growing up in the Midwest, Mandy was the youngest of three. Our early conversations told me what she liked: sports, Christmas, warm weather, pizza, chocolate, and root beer. Oh, and the color pink, which I could tell from her tennis shoes.

I liked her immediately and not just because she was giving Greg and me part of herself – literally. The lunches we shared in January, February, March, and April of that year were filled with conversations about TV shows, hobbies and, yes, the forthcoming adoption. Her parents and siblings supported her decision but most everyone else in her life didn't realize she spent her first year of college pregnant.

I'm thankful the open adoption provided another layer of support for Mandy. Hearing her talk about it years later was such a testimony to God's faithfulness:

"You all quickly turned into a wonderful support system for me through this time. I was away from most of my family and friends, and I was living a secret from almost everyone who knew me. It was a rough emotional situation on me. Once you all expressed the want to be involved in the doctor's appointments and delivery, I really didn't think about it much. I was able to detach my feelings for the baby and realize I was carrying a child for you."

A thank you note and the biggest care package would never do the trick. I can tell her time and time again I appreciated what she did and how she handled herself – not just for herself and her boyfriend, but for us and for Cate. I hope our girl has part of her determined spirit and positive attitude.

And then I can say it's in the genes.

When Mandy, Greg, and I gathered in a booth at a Bloomington restaurant, this brave teenager told us how she was grateful to have a plan after half a pregnancy of wondering what she should do. Years later, she reflected on the beginning of this process that would change both our lives:

"When I found out I was pregnant, I was in my first year of college, recovering from my battle with cancer and finding out what a 'normal' life for a 19-year-old was. My parents had offered to help me take care of the baby, if that is what I wanted, but I didn't. I wanted my child to grow up in a stable environment. I didn't want her to have to 'grow up with me.' In a way I was being selfish because I wanted to be able to experience the true college life – turning 21 and being able to go to a bar without wondering who I would get to babysit, choosing where I wanted to go to college, and freeing myself from my parents. The more I thought about my options of parenting her versus placing her for adoption, I knew this was another struggle God put in my life to overcome. That's when I knew I was going to find the best family to take care of my baby."

Mandy wanted this baby to have what she didn't think she could give her while still pursuing her college degree: the stability of two parents providing for her. Knowing adoption made this possible brought Mandy peace, which she later described to me:

"As soon as the perfect situation dropped into my lap, I immediately was at peace with the situation. I knew this is what God planned for me and that you all were the perfect family. I was very excited to have a purpose in this situation, so when I met you I was excited. I was excited because I was able to provide you something you had been looking forward to for so long. I was also very excited about the fact that you all had a lot of your ideal plan already worked out. I really hadn't thought of every detail or what kind of adoption I even wanted. I just knew that you all were the ones and we could figure everything out. Through the whole process, I was able to lean on you all to help me with and talk about the details to make the adoption work out."

———

On the way home from our first trip to Bloomington, Greg and I named our girl. Catherine Anna. It was a name we'd long held as our favorite. Catherine after my mom Mary Catherine, who goes by Cathy. Anna after Greg's grandma. We'd call her Cate.

Turns out, as I later learned, Mandy's middle name is Catherine.

Names are a big deal to me. Perhaps because my name is often misspelled, which used to bother me. Seeing my name written countless times with an "-en" instead of an "-in" has made me more sensitive to making sure I spell other people's names correctly. My sources appreciated the attention to detail when I was a newspaper reporter. So you'd think I wouldn't have named my daughter Cate. Ironically, I'm also not a fan of nicknames, yet here I was choosing my daughter's nickname before she was born.

No matter our name, God knows us intimately. He knows our names – and he knows the person each name identifies. Our names are written on his hand (Isaiah 49:16) and God calls his sheep by name (John 10:3). Max Lucado spoke to me in the introduction to *When God Whispers Your Name*:

> "Quite a thought, isn't it? Your name on God's hand. Your name on God's lips. Maybe you've seen your name in some special places. On an award or diploma or walnut door. Or maybe you've heard your name from some important people – a coach, a celebrity, a teacher. But to think that your name is on God's hand and on God's lips ... my, could it be? Or perhaps you've never seen your name honored. And you can't remember when you heard it spoken with kindness. If so, it may be more difficult for you to believe that God knows your name. But he does. Written on his hand. Spoken by his mouth. Whispered by his lips. Your name."[2]

While thinking about names, God reminded me He's always working – from when my mom and dad named their first-born daughter to when I chose a name for my first-born child. He knows who we are and who we'll become. He knows our failures and wants to be glorified in our successes.

God called me to motherhood in his time. Little did I know, being called "Mom" would be a new name that would change my life.

———

As we waited and wondered, God worked.

During the time I was having all those blood tests and we were visiting an infertility specialist, God was orchestrating a story that made me a momma in a way I never expected.

---

[2] Lucado, Max. When God Whispers Your Name. Nashville: Thomas Nelson, 1994.

We still didn't know the ins and outs of adoption, but, even at the beginning, we knew this situation was right for us. People – some even close to us – asked how we could open our hearts to this method of having a family when there was always a chance Mandy, like any birth mom, could change her mind. Sure, I realized Mandy could change her mind, but I knew she wouldn't.

I had heard adoption horror stories and have since witnessed some friends walk through a few of their own. But that peace that surpassed all my understanding stayed with me as we journeyed through the adoption process. I just knew Mandy was in it with us. It may have sounded naïve, but it's what I knew in my heart because we got to know her, as a person and not just our daughter's birth mom.

The birth father, who was Mandy's high school boyfriend, supported the adoption plan once she committed to it. He signed what he needed to sign from California, where he was in college, and later voluntarily submitted his DNA to a lab. Under Indiana law, he signed before Cate was born, making his consent valid once Mandy signed after the birth.

Mandy considered adoption her only and best option.

> "The situation was just too perfect and nobody could deny this was my best option," Mandy said. "My boyfriend at the time thought that we should just erase the situation all together, but all of my morals and values told me that wasn't the right option for my well-being. Adoption was the best option for me and my support system at the time agreed."

After the first meeting and doctor's appointment with Mandy, I found an attorney in Indiana who brought in a social worker. We had a social worker in Kentucky prepare our home study necessary for the legal part of adoption. An attorney friend helped us finalize the adoption in our home state. I was happy to trade the medicine that's messed with my hormones and many vials of blood for the paperwork and phone calls.

In the following months, we readied our home and ourselves as we prepared a nursery and read books on parenting. I was getting ready to become a mom, finally.

About two months before Cate was born, Jaclyn asked me if I was nervous. I surprised myself with my answer: "I haven't thought to be nervous." Of course, I elaborated, I was excited, reflective, thankful, and focused. I thought about getting the right paperwork to the social worker and had plenty of questions to ask the attorney. I considered how to decorate her room and the best ways to balance work and motherhood. I registered for baby accessories and talked with my friends about what exactly I would need. (The Diaper Genie didn't make the cut.) But I hadn't thought to be nervous.

I started thinking about how to implement a sleeping and eating schedule for a newborn. I thought about how adoptive babies have different needs than biological children. I knew we were going to have to stay in Indiana for 3-10 days before we could truly bring Cate home, but I looked forward to that time – our time – in some Hoosier hotel room.

I wondered how soon she would sleep through the night or if she would hate her car seat. I daydreamed about what my first thought would be the first time I held her. I didn't want to miss a single detail of this beautiful experience.

When Jaclyn asked me if I was nervous, I flipped through the ever-growing list in my mind of all the logistics and emotions and responsibilities and possibilities and never felt nervous.

I'm pretty sure the lack of nervousness was the presence of peace.

God didn't give me my way in December 2004 because his way in May 2007 was even better than I could imagine. Less than nine months after I stopped trying to become pregnant, I got to hold my daughter.

———

My cell phone ring jolted me awake at 5:47 a.m. on Sunday, May 6. I'm not an early morning person, but I was thrilled to hear Mandy's voice when I answered.

"My water broke and I'm on the way to the hospital," she said.

Cate's bags had been packed for weeks, but somehow Greg and I hadn't packed our own clothes. This was only the beginning of parenthood, I soon realized. We managed to be out of the house by 6:30 a.m., ignoring the dirty dishes on the kitchen counter as we locked our back door. Little did I know, this would be the first of many times in my life as a mother that dirty dishes (or any other chore) would have to wait.

We were at the hospital by 12:10 p.m. to await Cate's arrival, which came about 14 hours after Mandy arrived there and called us. Mandy was amazing, even during the back pains and labor. It takes a brave woman to be generous, gracious, and strong when she's preparing to deliver a baby she believes was meant for someone else.

We were in the room when Cate was born, and saying I'm thankful for that experience is an understatement. People asked if being in there was strange, and I would have thought I'd say it was. But, like the whole adoption process, the birth experience was meant to be – something I can only say because the Creator of the world orchestrated all the details for it to happen, leaving us with the peace that surpasses all my understanding, even during this intimate moment. We saw our eight-pound, twenty-inch girl as soon as she entered the world.

Cate had some inconsistent breathing at first, so they put on her the smallest oxygen mask I've ever seen. We watched as they cleaned her up and tended to her. She gripped our fingers. Then they took her to the nursery and kept her on oxygen for a short time.

Finally at 4 o'clock in the morning, the nurse brought our daughter to us. I fed her and then held her for three straight hours. Those were the moments for which I've been waiting. And, goodness, were they worth it.

And you know I'm not even a morning person.

On that first day of our girl's life, we spent some time with her and then took care of some adoption paperwork when the attorney came to the hospital. That's when Mandy held Cate. I didn't realize at the time how meaningful seeing them together would be for me. I'm grateful I have a picture that documents the moment Cate shared with her birth mom. Of course, those moments in the hospital room together weren't simple. Mandy knew she was beginning to transition back to "normal" life. We agreed that day I would share pictures and updates of Cate. Mandy and I later became Facebook friends.

What happened that day in the hospital room was only the beginning of a grieving process for Mandy:

> "The part that scared me the most was signing all the papers in the hospital with the lawyer. I was in such a daze after delivery and almost living in a surreal world. I remember thinking, 'I don't know what all I'm signing, but I hope it's the right choice.' I don't think I grieved until many years later. I think the open adoption helps with my need to grieve."

Greg and I were surprised when the pediatrician said we could leave as long as we got the required newborn screen within a couple of days. The hospital received the legal order that gave us temporary guardianship until the adoption could be finalized, and we were on our way as a family of three.

To comply with the Interstate Compact on the Placement of Children (ICPC), we couldn't leave Indiana to return home to Kentucky until both states cleared us. Despite technology, paperwork had to be filed and documented and then overnighted back and forth between the two capitals. We just had to wait. With family and friends in Louisville, Kentucky, we decided to go as close to the river as we could go to be near them. We were off to Jeffersonville, Indiana, with our baby girl just shy of 24 hours old.

Talk about a dream come true.

So much had changed in a day. I immediately got less sleep than I preferred, but I wouldn't have changed a thing. The nurse helped us tighten the straps on the car seat holding our newborn baby girl and we pulled away from that hospital with the greatest blessing God had ever given us.

We made a pit stop about a half hour down the road for dinner. And, yes, Cate's first diaper change outside the hospital happened at an Arby's in Columbus, Indiana. Another sixty-five miles down the road, we took up temporary residence in a hotel just a couple miles on the Indiana side of the Ohio River.

We stayed there seven nights. My mom brought us food. Friends came by with gifts to unwrap and gifts of their presence. We ate out many meals. (Thank God it wasn't flu season because I'm not sure we could have stayed confined to that hotel room for all those days!) Other than washing bottles, our chores were left at home. We really got to be a family for the first time without the pressures of daily life encroaching.

Even with a week-old baby in my arms, the newness seemed comfortable, like God had planned this for us. For months and months, I begged to be pregnant, but God heard the desire of my heart, which was to have a family. It's a lesson I still hold close: God sees beyond our words and knows our hearts' true desires. In his timing, we see a glimpse of his masterpiece.

In Their Words :: Allie Paschall

I've wanted to be a momma for as long as I can remember. I played with baby dolls longer than most girls, started babysitting at a young age, and even took a job as a full-time nanny for a couple years. I felt as if I was put on this earth to have lots of babies.

After marrying my high school sweetheart at 20 years old, we both knew we wanted children soon. We never used anything to prevent pregnancy, and after two years of nothing I went to my doctor with questions. I was quickly diagnosed with polycystic ovarian syndrome and a thyroid disease. The two together would make it near impossible to conceive naturally. I remember sobbing the entire hour's drive home.

My husband I had always kind of had adoption on the back burner. We loved the idea of adopting, but we thought it might be a way we completed our family, not begin it. As a young couple we just expected to get pregnant. We were wrong. We began fertility treatments and visits to specialists and, as we kept hearing "nos," we slowly began to hear God's "yes."

I'll never forget being in bed crying one night when my husband got home. It had just been a hard day of feeling alone. Baby showers, baby announcements, and baby births were the season of life most of our friends were in, and it was hard for me. I was sobbing and my husband walked over to me lying in the bed and whispered, "I'm ready to begin the adoption process when you are." And we began the next day! I have never felt so much peace, anticipation, hope, and joy. It was like it just "clicked" for both of us, and we never looked back.

We welcomed home a happy, healthy baby girl in September 2015. She changed our lives in so many ways. When I look at her every day, I am reminded adoption was never God's Plan B for our family. It was always His Plan A, and I'm so thankful that truth was revealed to us.

Allie Paschall has a love for her gracious Heavenly Father, farmer husband, baby girl, interior design, party hosting, and connecting people through adoption.

In Their Words :: Makenzie Shrewcraft

After several years of infertility, we set out on our adoption journey. We had always planned to adopt internationally later down the road, but after a little bit of research, we began looking into domestic adoption through an agency. I wasn't sold on the idea of an open adoption in the beginning, but our agency really encouraged it.

We began to pray about it and agreed to the possibility of openness with a birth mother. Somewhere along the way, my heart shifted. My prayers began to change from just begging for a baby to asking God to bring a birth mother into our lives.

Fast forward to a year later and we found out we had been chosen by Kathleen, a birth mother due with a baby girl in two months. She didn't want to meet us at the time, so we wrote her a letter and sent it through the agency. A few weeks later, our social worker called to say Kathleen was ready to meet with us in person.

At this point, it was 29 days before her induction date. That meeting went better than we could have ever imagined! We talked, laughed, and cried together, and we learned that Kathleen was someone who makes you feel like you've known her for years. She even looked down at her belly and said, "She is yours ... I'm just carrying her for you." From there, God gave us an undeniable peace the baby girl she was carrying was our daughter and Kathleen wouldn't change her mind about her adoption plan.

I prayed for Kathleen every day between the meeting and the day our daughter Gracen was born. I couldn't begin to imagine the emotions she was experiencing. When we arrived at the hospital, Gracen had just been born. Because of Kathleen's requests, we were planning to meet Gracen by ourselves but the pregnancy counselor met us and said she was in the room with Kathleen. It wasn't what we expected and we were a little nervous to be introduced to our daughter in front of her, but we walked in and she greeted us with a big "Hey!" and a smile. We ended up spending three hours in the room with Kathleen, holding Gracen in our arms. We talked about families, Kathleen's pregnancy, our hopes and dreams for Gracen, and what her room looked like at home. It was nothing like we planned and imagined, but it's time I would never change.

Even though Kathleen didn't want much contact with us after birth, our relationship began to grow. We began to email, which led to Facebook messaging, which eventually led to texting. We have only seen her once, right after Gracen's second birthday, but we keep in touch regularly. Although we talk about Gracen often, we also just chat about life, from jobs to family and everything in between. She is a dear friend in our lives.

Our adoption journey looked nothing like I thought it would. It was a pretty smooth process, which was a big blessing, but the daughter we brought home and the birth mother and friend we gained are two of the greatest people in our lives. We prayed for them long before we met them and God exceeded our expectations.

Makenzie Shrewcraft is wife to Brett, mommy to Gracen, and a wedding photographer in western Kentucky.

How God Chooses & Calls Us

For he chose us in him before the creation of the world to be holy and blameless in his sight. In love he predestined us for adoption to sonship through Jesus Christ, in accordance with his pleasure and will — to the praise of his glorious grace, which he has freely given us in the One he loves. ... In him we were also chosen, having been predestined according to the plan of him who works out everything in conformity with the purpose of his will, in order that we, who were the first to put our hope in Christ, might be for the praise of his glory. ... When you believed, you were marked in him with a seal, the promised Holy Spirit, who is a deposit guaranteeing our inheritance until the redemption of those who are God's possession — to the praise of his glory.

(Ephesians 1:4-7, 11, 13-14)

I never thought to tell the receptionist we were in the process of adopting Cate when I made her appointment at the local health department to get her four-month immunizations. While checking her in the morning of her appointment, I realized I didn't have the necessary paperwork, most importantly the court order giving us guardianship until Cate's adoption was finalized. Honestly, I never thought to bring it to prove Cate was my daughter even though she didn't officially share my last name yet.

She had been my daughter since she was born, but in reality, well, at least from the government's perspective, it wasn't official. While the health department may be cheaper than the pediatrician's office for immunizations with our health insurance, there's a bit more red tape to maneuver without getting stuck. I reminded myself I was saving at least $100 – even though it required another appointment the following week with the proper paperwork.

We had to wait on the legal process before Cate could have our last name. I had to prove to the health department she was mine. The whole adoption process gives me perspective on how God adopts us.

Before I knew God, He chose me. Because He chose me, glorious grace is poured into my everyday life and an inheritance is prepared for me. Read Ephesians 1:11 from The Message: "It's in Christ that we find out who we are and what we are living for. Long before we first heard of Christ and got our hopes up, he had his eye on us, had designs on us for glorious living, part of the overall purpose he is working out in everything and everyone." Other translations of that verse say we were chosen (NIV), we are united with Christ (NLT), we were made a heritage (ASV), and we have obtained an inheritance (ESV).

We are family. I get that. I didn't grow Cate in my womb, but we prepared for her and embraced her from the beginning. Greg and I named her and prayed for her before we held her in our arms. We're grateful for Mandy, who chose life for her, and that God chose her for us.

Cate didn't have to do anything to be our child. She's named in our will and was called daughter long before the court recognized her new birth certificate. We chose her in the beginning and we have chosen her every day since. Likewise, God chose me in the beginning and still chooses me today – even when I stumble.

Jesus says people will know we are in His family by our love. Of course, sometimes I don't do a good job of representing my eternal family name. But this truth is my foundation. And it's why I was surprised when the health department wanted me to produce some piece of paper to prove Cate was my daughter.

That and many other adoption-related papers lived in a file at home. Not long after, I received another piece of paper that made our reality official. Yes, it was just a piece of paper, but I had waited so long to become a mom that I was relieved when the court considered me one too.

About a week after I became a stay-at-home mom when Cate was four months old, we had our final adoption hearing in the local court, where we knew the judge, considered our attorney our friend, and knew the bailiffs by name, thanks to our jobs. While addressing the judge, I accidentally called him by his first name because that's how I'd known him months earlier when I wrote a newspaper article about his campaign to be elected the first family court judge in our small town. Our attorney stopped the hearing at one point to take a picture of Cate because she apparently looked especially cute laying on my lap chewing on the stuffed bear the court clerk had given her.

At our next immunization appointment, I proudly told the health department receptionist her name was now officially Catherine Anna Taylor – and, yes, I had a court order to prove it.

———

I was away from my newsroom desk for six weeks after Cate was born.

My baby girl had a mess of dark hair and long fingers and toes. People often said, "Oh, those long fingers, maybe she'll play the piano." Greg has hopes she can palm a basketball. Keeping with the hardwood dream, early on he taught her the modified Kentucky Wildcats cheer that works well with her name. C-A-T-E. Cate. Cate. Cate.

We didn't plan that (or the fact her initials spell CAT), but it's a sure way to keep the Hoosier out of her. She really was a Kentucky girl from the beginning. Of course, you have to be a college basketball fan to understand that Wildcat-Hoosier rivalry.

While I was away from my job, three city council meetings were officially in the minutes as I read three novels, usually with Cate by my side. In the 504 hours (including weekends) that I was off work, Cate gained two pounds, bringing her to double-digit weight and moving her up a diaper size.

I left my six-week-old girl home with Greg and I went back to the newsroom in the mornings when my leave was complete. Working at a newspaper that published in the afternoon meant the mornings were hopping. Afternoons were less busy and my bosses let me work at home after lunch. I made phone calls and sent emails, typed stories, and even toted the baby carrier around to informal interviews while Greg went into his office. This arrangement worked well – at least until Cate was mobile.

I wasn't eager to go back to the job I loved. Six weeks as a momma changed me. But I went back – mostly because I said I would and I needed the health insurance. So back and forth we went, often eating lunch together – our family of three – before one of us went out of the door again. I wondered if this coming and going was really going to be best, but I plugged along and dismissed wonders of what kind of mom I would be if I didn't have to balance it with a full-time job with sometimes strange hours.

After six weeks back on the job, I really thought about the reality of quitting my job – something my husband had posed before Cate was even born. I didn't see myself as a stay-at-home mom, so I hadn't really considered it an option until this point. Greg was thrilled I was entertaining the idea and I was immediately thankful he didn't push me to stay home even though it would have been his preference from the beginning.

We figured out how to get me health insurance. A diabetic needs insurance, yet the chronic condition can be considered a pre-existing condition, creating hurdles for someone like me trying to get insured. After getting insurance, I gave my editor a month's notice that I was leaving. It surprised him slightly less than when I phoned in my last-minute request to be off work to meet Mandy about eight months earlier.

Growing up with parents who worked for the local school system and brought home paychecks every other week, giving up my consistent paycheck seemed risky, even with Greg's efforts to continue growing his law practice well beyond my reporter's salary. We were a year into Greg's self-employment when I told my editor I was leaving. Being my Type-A self who likes the checkbook balanced to the penny, this all made me nervous when I thought too much about the financial aspect. Even so, in my heart, I knew it was right.

God's peace surpassed my understanding again. That provision would have been enough, but then God also provided for us in a financial way we weren't expecting. In addition to practicing law, Greg and his dad had a real estate business of buying, renovating, and selling homes, often ones that were nearing foreclosure. One of those properties sold in March 2007. As the adoption bills came in later that summer, we realized that sale alone would cover the cost of Cate's adoption.

————

Leaving the newsroom had me thinking about my name again. People say there is much in a name. Mine had often been misspelled, but I haven't always been known by my name alone.

My elementary school label of "Mr. Hill's daughter" wore off as I grew older. But growing up in a small town with a principal as a father and a teacher as mother, being the educators' daughter was how I was known. The label may have contributed to my shyness because I worried I would mess up and disappoint – and my dad was my elementary school principal.

In middle school I started developing a slightly independent identity. But then in high school my aunt was my English teacher both my junior and senior years. I never addressed her by name because I wasn't sure whether to call her Aunt Carolyn or Mrs. Godbey. Either way, other students knew I was "Mrs. Godbey's niece." And just so you know, I got a B in Advanced Placement English at least one of the quarters, so I didn't breeze through my aunt's class.

When I wasn't deciding how to get my aunt's attention those two years, I was in the newspaper office. I spent my senior year as high school newspaper editor, a role that prompted another identity – "Newspaper Editor" – but more importantly served as a springboard to college. When I got to Murray State, hardly anyone knew my name, but I found "The Murray State News." I spent those four years learning about myself. Despite five year's difference in age, my sister and I grew closer. I solidified my love for writing, especially to inform and educate. I made friends I intended to keep for my lifetime. And I met the guy who would become my husband. My collegiate roles were varied, and the labels fewer.

Eight months after I graduated from Murray State, I became Greg's fiancée. And then six months after that, I changed my last name to Taylor. We – now collectively "The Taylors" – spent our first year in Lexington, where we started finding our identity as a couple. Then we moved to Murray, where we've been since August 2003.

Murray is his hometown, but it's also the hometown of our relationship. This is where we met, and this is where we settled. We started our family here and made big decisions about our careers here.

Early on in our time in Murray, I assumed another identity: "Kristin at the Ledger." In my four years there, I wrote at least 2,175 stories. And that doesn't include all the court news and police logs I compiled. I laid out pages, snapped pictures, answered more phone calls than I could even tally, and filled in for my editor more than once.

But most of the work in this job happens outside the office, building relationships and learning the community. I covered eighty-eight city council meetings and two murder trials. Each month, I covered regular meetings at city hall, Murray State, Murray-Calloway County Hospital, and CrimeStoppers. And along the way, I kept up with criminal court cases and state politics. Truth be told: I liked my job, my professional identity, more than I ever thought I would. I was pleasantly surprised with the way I became part of the community.

Even so, I knew replacing my pen and notebook with bottles and naptimes was the right thing for me. Cate was only four months old at the time, but she'd already changed me. I fully embraced my new identity as "Cate's mom," starting officially after I finished writing about Murray State University's Board of Regents on my last day as a reporter.

There is much in a name. But there is more to be said about purpose and the way God provides.

————

Possibly the most ironic part of the health department needing proof she was mine in the beginning was all the other people who have since told me how much we resemble each other. God surprised me over and over again in the best ways throughout Cate's adoption process, but one of the biggest visible surprises was Cate herself. With an Iranian birth father, we expected her to have olive-toned skin.

Instead people debate whether she looks most like Greg or me. We both have blue eyes; she has gorgeous brown eyes that soak up details. She's always had defined eyes, which seem to have come from her birth father who we've never met. Cate tans well and has always had dark hair. It's lightened some in recent years, making it closer to Mandy's hair color.

When people comment on how she looks like me, I pause for a moment because I want to tell them her story, our story. We may not share DNA, but I'm raising a mini-me who was meant to be my daughter.

The similarities go beyond looks. Cate and I are both stereotypical first-borns. She is stubborn, tells detailed stories, likes crafts, loves her friends, wants to have a plan, and has perfectionist tendencies – just like me.

And yet she's not like me, especially as a child. She's not afraid of most new things, speaking in front of people doesn't scare her, she laughs easily, and she wants to play sports. I'm more adventurous as an adult than I ever was as a kid. She makes me proud the way she faces life.

I welcome the similarities because I didn't expect them with adoption. Maybe it's our common dark brown hair that prompts people to say she looks like me. Perhaps it's the skin tone. But it could be the ways she behaves like me. She likes to make her friends cards, especially when they're sad or sick. She likes to help me in the kitchen. She likes to take (and plan!) road trips. And each night before she goes to bed, she asks me what we're doing the next day.

Sometimes I catch myself scolding her for behavior that's just like mine. Ouch. I see my weaknesses in her and cringe, not because she disappoints me but because I disappoint myself and I know she's watching. We both get cranky when we're tired and have been known to break when our plans break.

I watch her live and laugh and write and play and imagine and worry and ponder and plan. And I know that even in my imperfect perfectionist-leaning mothering ways, this girl is one of the best things that's ever happened to me.

Throughout the years, I'm often reminded how Cate – and our other kids who followed – belong in our family. In the fall of 2016, Cate came home from fourth grade full of frustration. It was the same day I listened to "Be Kind to Yourself" by Andrew Peterson for the first time. That song – starting with the title alone – spoke truth into my house and my heart.

> "You can't expect to be perfect / It's a fight you've gotta forfeit / You belong to me whatever you do / So lay down your weapon, darling / Take a deep breath and believe that I love you / Be kind to yourself"[3]

That afternoon, Cate misplaced a folder with a paper she was supposed to return to school. I know the frustration of knowing you had something but not remembering where you last had it. She was also still missing her best friend who unexpectedly didn't return that year to the school they had shared, and that grief was fresh after a FaceTime conversation earlier in the week. Plus she'd had a little conflict with another classmate during recess.

The frustrations are different for each one of us. We misplace things, overact in our responses to people we love, wish circumstances would change, long for a different season of life, and become overwhelmed with the details of daily life.

Conflicting emotions can rise up when you least expect them. I know how those situations can echo in your heart and the replays often make it worse. Like me, many of Cate's frustrations came from the battles within herself. I fight some of those internal battles myself, so I know the burdens they create. I know the same frustrations that were on her mind that afternoon – or any other afternoon. I know how being tired magnifies them. I know the personal expectations that are ridiculous and distract from what matters.

---

[3] Peterson, Andrew. Be Kind To Yourself. Centricity Music, 2015.

It's easy to listen to emotions and lies and expectations. But it's more important to listen to truth. Andrew Peterson's song encompassed a message I've spent years trying to digest. It's the same truth I want my girl – regardless of her age – to hear in her heart and mind when those emotions well up and things are misplaced.

Be kind to yourself. Forfeit the fight to be perfect. Listen to God's truth.

With that message, I think about society and how we hand out participation trophies and tell girls they can be anything they want. That all sounds good – until we've raised a generation that doesn't know how to lose and doesn't recognize that we're all created as individuals with different skills and talents.

At nine years old, Cate was already taller than most Olympic gymnasts, so why would I tell her she can be anything she wants when I know she's not going to become a gymnast or a jockey?

We can't all be anything and everything. We need to be who God created us as individuals to be, always giving our best but recognizing this world doesn't revolve around us.

Adoption reminds me we are chosen and called for reasons we understand better as we draw nearer to our Creator.

God knew when I cried out to him to become pregnant that we would have this story.

A decade after we learned about Cate, I was unpacking boxes from our family's move when a 2006 scrapbook distracted me. I had forgotten all about a letter I'd written to my future baby about what God had taught me through the wait to become a momma. I declared I'd name a baby girl Catherine Anna and listed possibly boy names we never did use. But the best detail? The letter was written in August – about the same time Mandy conceived Cate.

God knew when I scribbled that letter that I would come back to it a decade later and be amazed at His faithfulness. God knew He was going to make us a family through adoption – through THIS adoption. God knew her brown eyes because He created them. He created every single one of her eye lashes and every hair on her head. He knew how she would laugh and that her stories would be long. He knew how we would fit together.

She's taught me nurture trumps nature because biologically speaking she wasn't created within me. But I know without a doubt she was created to be my daughter. I understand her. I yearned for her. I learn from her every day. Her story is my story because through it God rescued my heart.

His works are indeed wonderful. Seems official to me.

In Their Words :: Jennifer Jackson Linck

I learned an amazing lesson about sacrifice from my friend's 13-year-old daughter as we prepared for a garage sale to continue working toward our goal of $18,000 to adopt our son, Jackson.

My friend Elizabeth called me after she dropped off donations for the garage sale.

"Inside one of the boxes is a small plastic bag with money in it," she said. "Morgan wanted to donate the money she has been saving to your adoption fund."

I choked back tears thinking of Morgan's sacrifice for a child she didn't know. I found the plastic bag and pulled out the most precious and meaningful $15 I had ever received. The donation meant more than any other gift we received because of the heart of the giver.

Morgan had given everything she had without wanting anything in return.

I was reminded of the widow's offering in Luke 24. The rich were putting extravagant gifts into the temple treasury. Jesus, however, wasn't moved by the extreme gifts. What caught His eye was the widow who placed two small copper coins into the treasury as an offering. Jesus said, "This poor widow has put in more than all the others. All these people gave their gifts out of their wealth; but she out of her poverty put in all she had to live on."

After Morgan offered such a beautiful sacrifice on our behalf, I felt the Lord asking me what I was willing to sacrifice to meet the financial needs of our adoption.

With each Bible study I completed, each sermon I heard or book I read, a common theme remained: sacrifice. God didn't want me to find my security in the things of the world. He wanted me to be willing to step out of my comfort zone. How could I be more like Morgan? Would I give everything I had for the sake of my child?

Jennifer Jackson Linck is the author of "Bringing Home the Missing Linck: A Journey of Faith to Family" and "Jackson Finds His Voice," a children's book about Childhood Apraxia of Speech, who blogs at www.jenniferjacksonlinck.com.

How God Made Us Four

Remember how the Lord your God led you all the way in the wilderness ...
to humble and test you in order to know what was in your heart, whether or not you
would keep his commands. ... Observe the commands of the Lord your God, walking
in obedience to him and revering him. For the Lord your God is bringing you into a good
land — a land with brooks, streams, and deep springs gushing out into the valleys and
hills; ... a land where bread will not be scarce and you will lack nothing ...

(Deuteronomy 8:2, 6-7, 9)

Adopting a second child was a continuation of the story God was writing in our family.

In October 2008, we took the first step toward adopting a second child. I mailed a book about our family to a friend who works in labor and delivery. We didn't have a timeline because even my stubborn heart had learned that was pointless, but we wanted to put it out there – out to whoever would happen upon my blog, read a Facebook post, or engage in an adoption-related conversation – that we were ready to expand our family.

Or at least we thought we were ready.

Even then, when Cate was just eighteen months old, I enjoyed reminiscing about the details of how God made us a family. Adoption certainly is a process. For me, Cate's adoption was also a faith journey and I sensed God wasn't done yet.

Looking back on the peace I learned when I stopped trying to get pregnant, I never once felt like I settled for something less by not birthing a biological child. I didn't feel like I missed out by not being pregnant. I felt free not having to wonder why my body didn't make the right amounts of the right hormones or whether this month was the month our imperfect bodies would create life.

Infertility was the hardest journey I'd personally experienced. The Israelites spent forty years wandering through the wilderness, hoping for The Promised Land. Thankfully, our hard season wasn't that long, but infertility was my wilderness. Like the Israelites, I complained and faced obstacles along the way but ended up being refined through the journey that taught me God is faithful to His people and His promises.

It's impossible to find regret in that. Only hope.

And we hoped God would make us a family of four.

———

Because of that wilderness, the process to adopt was different the second time around. In April 2009, I started gathering paperwork to update our home study. I didn't have to start from scratch this time and I knew a little more of what to expect. The emotions were fewer and the urgency less this time. Yes, the desire was there, but we didn't have the same kind of time to dwell on it as we lived life with our daughter who was about to turn two.

At that time I studied *A Woman's Heart* by Beth Moore with some ladies at church, learning about the Israelites' experience building the Tabernacle and drawing parallels to the ways God dwells in his believers. God wanted the earthly Tabernacle to be a replica of a heavenly plan, so much so He instructed the Israelites how to build things, where to put them, and how to decorate them. Yes, our God is someone who appreciates and notices details. Even knowing what God had done for us through Cate's adoption, I clung to Beth Moore's words:

"God is detailed. He is not a God of generalities. He is a God of individuality. Do not let Satan convince you that God is not actively involved in the intricate design of your life. God has not missed a single stitch or left a stone unturned on your behalf; furthermore, His activity in the details of your life most often displays His glory and beauty."[4]

The same God builds families. He has different ways of doing so, but He's the master planner of them all. And God has been in the business of making families for many generations. Beth Moore commented in one of the Bible study videos that every time God makes childlessness an issue in the Bible as He did with Elizabeth, Hannah and Sarah, He is preparing his people for a miracle.

Every time.

Pregnancy comes easily to so many people – some of whom take the life inside of them for granted. But Beth Moore gave me new perspective on this: This thing that comes so naturally to some came supernaturally to Greg and me. I was chosen to become a mom this way and in the process witnessed God's glory in a unique way.

Like Elizabeth said in Luke 1:25, "The Lord has done this for me." I wondered how I would see God's glory the next time.

———

On Cate's second birthday, we met with the same social worker who had originally completed our home study to update it for what we assumed would be an agency adoption. We loved everything about Cate's independent, private adoption process. And, really, we wanted to do it that way again, but we assumed we should proceed with the "normal" adoption route.

[4] Moore, Beth. A Woman's Heart: God's Dwelling Place. Nashville: LifeWay Press, 2007.

Yes, I know, what's normal about adoption processes? Somehow I still thought I was in charge of the plan, at least a little bit. Obviously, that's a lesson I learn over and over again in my life. God knows best, it's true.

So in May 2009, we chose an agency in Fort Worth, Texas, and made plans to attend an orientation there in July – because we already had an extended family vacation planned to the Lone Star State. I filled out grant applications, gathered documents for our home study, and made an appointment to meet with our local attorney to update him on our desire to adopt again. That last matter was important because I'd already put his name on countless forms.

More evidence of life not being what I expected, our attorney called a couple days after we met with him to tell us he found us a birth mom. Well, actually, the birth mom found him and he thought of us.

I couldn't even orchestrate this miraculous timing if I tried. And Lord knows I tried.

A local, pregnant, unmarried woman who was twenty-five years old, worked full time, and was going back to school wanted a family to adopt her baby boy who was due at the beginning of December.

Yes! Really? Maybe. Wait …

We were supposed to leave on Saturday for Texas, where our itinerary included meeting with an adoption agency that seemed like a perfect fit for us. Yet the Monday before we were to leave I talked to a woman who was pregnant with a boy who needed a family.

We sat on a couch in her living room the night before we left for Texas and discussed how adoption could work. The baby she was carrying was due about the same time her son turned one. Leigh reflected years later about how she believed adoption was the best plan – both for the son she was raising and the one growing inside her:

"I chose adoption because at that point and time in my life I knew there was no way I could financially support two children. Plus the father of the child said he was not going to help me in any way. I knew making an adoption plan for baby would give him a better chance at having a good life with more opportunities."

We left her house that was about seven miles from ours believing she was committed to her decision, but we hadn't talked with the birth father yet and had one hesitation: We live in a typical small town, where people know each other's business. We love our adoption stories – and we love telling our adoption stories. But some details of adoption don't need to be tossed around small-town gossip circles – or even among my husband's large extended family that has lived here for generations. Leigh was on the same page, uninterested in small-town drama.

We met with the agency anyway, but the more we talked about it the more clear our decision seemed to be. Conversations and prayers led to peace, erasing our hesitation. When we returned from Texas, we proceeded with this second independent, private adoption we weren't expecting but were thrilled to embrace.

We meet Leigh at her next appointment and saw our son via ultrasound on August 11, 2009. He was twenty-five weeks in his birth mother's womb and weighed one pound, seven ounces – so much like his big sister's storyline.

Only God does something like that.

Like Cate, we thought we'd name him after someone in our family, but we couldn't settle on the nickname version of Greg's grandpa, William, who went by Bill – the one we thought we'd honor. Greg wanted a Bill; I wanted a Will. So we went to the Bible instead of our family trees and agreed on Benjamin. His middle name – Lucas – is my grandpa's middle name.

We continued meeting Leigh for doctor's appointments. "We" usually meant two-year-old Cate and me. Conversations with Leigh were easy even though I know making an adoption plan was hard on her momma heart. In Greg and me, Leigh found what she wanted for this baby boy – financially secure, religious, well-rounded people, in her words:

"Having you two involved in the latter part of pregnancy was very important to me and helped me with the decision of adoption," Leigh told me as she reflected on the adoption more than four years later. "It made me feel better getting to know the two of you more and being able to accept that this was the right decision I was making."

Leigh's dad and stepmom as well as others in her life were supportive of her decision and kind to Greg and me when we briefly met. We also found an ally in the obstetrician, who was a family friend of ours and had taken Leigh and our unborn baby under his care. "My family and everyone in my life at that time supported me of my decision, which made the whole process much easier," Leigh reminisced. "I was happy to have that support system."

Adoption had blessed our family once and God was doing it again, in some of the same ways and in plenty of different ways. In the end, God's faithfulness remained and He covered our lives with the peace that surpasses anything we can truly understand.

———

Greg and I don't really do one thing at a time. As we prepared for Ben to be born, we also moved to a new-to-us house just across town and potty-trained Cate. But guess what? I really wouldn't have it any other way. God strung together all the events and their timing. And he sustained his peace in my life. I read a quote from Beth Moore in "The Patriarchs" that gave me pause: "Few things define us more than how we struggle. When we struggle through the crisis with God all the way to the blessing, we are gloriously redefined."[5]

---

[5] Moore, Beth. The Patriarchs: Encountering the God of Abraham, Isaac, and Jacob. Nashville: LifeWay Press, 2005.

I'm not always a good struggler. I verbalize my frustrations. And sometimes I talk harshly to those I love most. But having come through the infertility crisis with new life – both in my heart and with a baby girl added to my family – I understood that struggles shape us and prepare us for what's coming our way.

Each time God let me struggle, He also covered my mistakes with grace and gave me opportunities to embrace who I was (and, really, still am) becoming. For me, nothing has been more sanctifying than becoming a mom.

And I was about to become a mom to two.

———

While we were camping with relatives on Saturday, November 21, 2009, my sister-in-law Angela asked me what my perfect timing would be for Ben's birth. Leigh had been on bed rest because he'd threatened to come early, so we were glad he was still inside growing at more than thirty-eight weeks. I answered Angela's question honestly: Sunday or Monday.

Well, Monday started with me going with Leigh to a check-up appointment. We learned she was five to six centimeters dilated. Given that she had initially dilated two months earlier, we were happy to be just eight days from his due date. Our doctor friend was confident he'd deliver our son soon and wanted Leigh to get ready for delivery.

Turns out, he was right.

After Leigh and I each gathered things from our houses and made childcare arrangements, we met at the hospital. That was about 11 o'clock that morning. A couple hours later, the doctor broke her water.

Benjamin Lucas was born November 23, 2009, three blocks from our house. His sister, who was almost thirty-one months old, was thrilled to welcome him into our family. Once again God knew the desires of our heart and fulfilled them in His time. He showed us His faithfulness in such a tangible way. This time it came into the world at 2:56 p.m. the Monday before Thanksgiving, weighing seven pounds, ten ounces and with a head full of dark hair.

Leigh was a champ. She held my hand during delivery, but she rarely really squeezed it. She never complained and told me thank you a couple of times.

No, thank you. Really, that's all I kept thinking. THANK YOU, Leigh. THANK YOU, God.

Once Ben was born, the nurse took him to a neighboring room to clean him up, which was Leigh's preference. After hugging Leigh multiple times, Greg and I followed the nurse, who carried our son. She tended to him and then we held him. This great nurse even was good with the camera and took a picture that turned out to my favorite from the day.

Even with the celebration, I knew there was heartache for Leigh:

"I grieved as any mother would do after delivery and losing her child. It was a feeling of being torn apart because even though I knew it was the right decision, it was still hard to let him go. I cried for many days and still do every now and then, but I still know it was the right thing and wouldn't change my decision for anything," Leigh said years later. "I think that adoption is a great idea for any mother who might have reservations about having a child at a bad time in their life. I've never believed in abortion, and to give someone a child that might not be able to have one or that might be able to give them better opportunities in life is wonderful."

The nursing staff arranged for us to have a room, so we went there while the nursery staff did the things they do to newborns. A nurse who had been Greg's elementary school bus driver years earlier brought Ben to us and then Greg's parents brought Cate to meet her brother.

———

Before we could leave the hospital, we had a slight adoption snafu. We learned the court wanted a different type of paperwork than what our attorney had pre-filed. By now it was the Tuesday before Thanksgiving and I was determined not to be stuck in the hospital while judges took an extended holiday. Greg spent much of that day on the phone with another attorney in our original attorney's office. We visited Leigh to get some different papers signed and took a trip to the courthouse in the neighboring county, where the family court judge was working that day. He was the same judge I called by his first name in Cate's final adoption hearing.

We secured the paperwork we needed and were glad to bring Ben home when he was twenty-five hours old. Perhaps the upcoming holiday worked in our favor, despite the paperwork snafu.

Our first family outing came on Ben's fourth day of life. We celebrated Thanksgiving at my in-laws' house. The people who had colds didn't touch our newborn son while my mother-in-law cooked a turkey that was almost three times Ben's weight. I'm sure he enjoyed feasting on his formula-filled bottles.

———

My kids have baby books like any other kid. I glued down pictures of their nurseries and ultrasound images and filled out their first words, monthly weights and heights, and what was popular the years they were born. But those baby books don't have spaces for their adoption stories. And those adoptions stories definitely deserve documentation.

I took the pages from the traditional baby books and combined them with pages of my own into a three-ring binder. Any good story needs a name, right?

Like Cate's own name, her adoption book title came easily. Chosen. Just like those verses from Ephesians I talked about earlier. I named the book before I filled it with content.

Ben's book was filled with content and I still was brainstorming a title. Words aren't Greg's love language like they are mine, but I went to my husband for suggestions. He rattled off a few that weren't meaningful enough to me. I bugged him about it again later and he said, "What about beloved?"

Beloved. Yes, that was it.

I wanted to incorporate a Bible verse, so I Googled scriptures that used "beloved." I skipped over several from Song of Solomon and then I read this from Deuteronomy 33:12: "About Benjamin he said: 'Let the beloved of the Lord rest secure in him, for he shields him all day long, and the one the Lord loves rests between his shoulders.'"

SERIOUSLY?! "About Benjamin ..." It couldn't have been more perfect. It's the message I want Ben to know. He can rest secure in the Lord, who protects him.

Not long after I put the finishing touches on Ben's adoption book and added the blessings some friends wrote him during our adoption finalization party we hosted to celebrate Ben when the whole thing was official on January 28, 2010. That's when I saw Deuteronomy 33:12 quoted on a blessing from our friend Nathan, who is the father to a boy less than a month older than Ben. The boys have been playmates since before they can remember and here was a blessing that echoed the same words to which God had led me.

God is definitely in the details and he remains faithful to show us His glory, sometimes in ways we never expect.

In Their Words :: Whitney Scott

We always knew we wanted to adopt one day regardless of whether we had biological children, but I always worried if I would love our adopted child how I loved our bio kids. Simple answer is YES! We have two biological children – Layna (born in 2009) and Ryder (2016) – and an adopted child – Nora (2015) – between them.

Nora was born via emergency C-section because of breathing complications so she was in the NICU for eight days. The original plan was to be at the hospital and see our birth mom before she was taken back, but Nora had other plans and was twelve hours old when we arrived at the hospital.

The NICU wasn't as scary as it could have been because we'd been there (in another hospital) with Layna, who was born at thirty weeks and spent eight weeks in the NICU. We were pros at the NICU life, but this time it was totally different: It almost felt like we were just visiting another baby instead of meeting our daughter for the first time. I began to feel guilty and worry that I wouldn't feel a connection to our newest daughter. Looking back, I realize that was just the devil.

We held Nora the day after her birth – and that is all it took! Holding her skin to skin, I felt like I had known her the entire past nine months she was growing. I wanted to hold her for hours and just bond with her, but that's not how life in the NICU works when nurses are helping a baby get her breathing under control. We held her any chance we could, whether it lasted two minutes or twenty. And we fell in love with her.

A few weeks later, we found out I was pregnant. Surprise! This was a complete shock and miracle in itself because of previous physical complications. Nora and Ryder are exactly nine months and one day apart because Ryder was born a week and a half late.

Having babies so close in age, I worried I couldn't love either of them enough. Once again the devil worked. Giving birth or adopting is really no different when it comes to love. I believe once you get to hold your baby for the first time it's all the same: You completely fall in love.

Adoption is different in one aspect because you also love your child's birth mom like no other relationship. Adoption is obvious in our family because our two youngest are so close in age, but Nora looks like our family. Just because I physically didn't birth her doesn't mean she is any less than my daughter than Layna is.

We always knew we wanted to adopt. Despite people's questions about why even though we can have biological kids, we hope to adopt again and are wondering if God is pointing us in the special needs direction. We can't wait to see how He writes our story!

Whitney Scott is a wife, mom, lover of Jesus, hairdresser, and makeup artist doing life the best she knows how.

How God Doesn't Leave Us the Same

Consider it pure joy, my brothers and sisters, whenever you face trials of many kinds because you know that the testing of your faith produces perseverance. Let perseverance finish its work so that you may be mature and complete, not lacking anything.

(James 1:2-4)

We all have roles to play in a story. Wife, mother, friend, sister, daughter, and aunt are the roles in which I'm regularly cast in my story. Many years ago, when my high school friends and I listened to Nirvana, Stone Temple Pilots, and Spin Doctors, I realized I didn't have to be a teacher like my dad, my mom, and my aunt. I began embracing the journalism world, first by writing for and then editing my high school newspaper. Then I went into college and eventually real-world newsrooms. I figured that's where I'd stay.

Then my baby girl gave me perspective. We are shaped by the other people in our story, regardless of how small in size they are.

My story doesn't have to be predictable and isn't going to unfold like I expect. But that's part of the thrill of turning the pages. *A Million Miles in a Thousand Years: What I Learned While Editing My Life* by Donald Miller gave me much to think about life, and how we write our stories moment by moment.

I'm glad I'm not the same person as I was when I listened to "Interstate Love Song." The soundtrack to my life would certainly be different now because I'm different now. That's how life is supposed to be. Like Miller says, "If the point of life is the same as the point of a story, the point of life is character transformation."[6]

We meet people along the way and those people help shape us. Almost as a direct result of quitting my job, I made two new friends. Courtney was a mom of two. Our husband have since become business partners – talk about the ripple effects of God not wasting anything in our lives. Holly was single and took my place at my desk in the newsroom I left. She moved on to other newsrooms, but she has loved my family since.

We might even get lost along the way. And that's okay too because finding our way back might mean we discover something beautiful. We hear songs, read books, laugh, cry, and see the sights as we travel to whatever is next.

Motherhood is the epitome of adventure for me.

Thankfully, we aren't alone in our stories. As I read Donald Miller's book in early 2010, the main characters in my story were my husband, my toddler daughter and my newborn son. We have friends and family who often show up in the pages of our lives. And through it all, we have roles to embrace. Because I'm a mom, I'll also teach my children about their roles in our family, in our community and in the world. They're going to learn regardless of whether I intentionally teach them, so I want to choose what I hope they learn.

It was eye-opening to watch Cate play her new role as Ben's big sister. She still takes that role seriously. When he was a baby, she didn't want Ben to cry and often checked on him. She picked out a baby blue blanket just like her beloved pink "nigh-night" and he's slept with it nearly every night since. We influence each other, even when we're small.

Having a toddler and newborn who constantly need me can be tiring. But I'm not in this story alone – thank God for that.

The early days of mothering two kids were hard for me.

---

[6] Miller, Donald. A Million Miles in a Thousand Years: What I Learned While Editing My Live. Nashville: Thomas Nelson, 2009.

Having two kids younger than three can be draining. Someone always needs something. A cup of juice. A bottle. A diaper change. A trip to the bathroom. A snack. A nap. Thank God one of the two was potty-trained.

People told me having two was much, much different than one. But I thought I had prepared. I organized my grocery list better. I planned when I would run errands around baby feeding times and clustered stops together so I could be more efficient. I clung to the advice of a friend: Remember you can lay Ben down and he won't go anywhere in those early months.

But I wasn't prepared for the emotional drain. I didn't wish to be anywhere else, but I cried often those early months of mothering two. Here I was with two precious miracles – my heart's desires – and I couldn't stop crying. Everyone needed something and I felt like I wasn't meeting anyone's needs. Ben spit up often and we spent time trying different formulas. I didn't want Cate to feel left out. Greg only got what leftovers I had mentally and physically. I felt helpless. And guilty.

Thankfully, the tears stopped. Plenty of days still leave me feeling ill-equipped to be a mom, but that drives me to the Maker.

For me, parenting is making a long-term investment in two people. These little people are going to become teenagers and then adults. Greg and I are responsible for shaping their childhood. We're responsible for making decisions that will affect their futures, both where they are and who they are.

No wonder it's not easy. Sometimes I would lose sight of the big picture, overwhelmed by minor frustrations, but knowing God chose these two for us helps me appreciate reality.

In Ben's first months of life, I filled sippy cups and bottles and I got to hear a sweet two-year-old voice imitate "I love you" and hand out unsolicited kisses. She even thanked me for washing her clothes and her favorite blanket.

We've taught Cate to say "please" and "thank you," to hold my hand when we're walking through a parking lot, and to be gentle with her brother. I've also noticed all the things I didn't realize I was teaching her: She likes cabinet doors to be closed. She puts things back where they belong. And she likes to be covered with a blanket while she sits on the couch to watch a movie. She gets every one of those things from me.

It all sounds mundane, but when my eyes are fixed on God it becomes more – just like Max Lucado writes in *The Applause of Heaven*:

> "Once again, the mundane became majestic. Once again the dull became the divine, the humdrum holy. Once again God's power was seen not through the ability of the instrument, but through its availability. 'Blessed are the meek,' Jesus explained. Blessed are the available. Blessed are the conduits, the tunnels, the tools. Deliriously joyful are the ones who believe that if God has used sticks, rocks and spit to do his will, then he can use us."[7]

One evening when Ben was two months old, Cate sat close to me feeding her baby doll. I asked Greg to take a picture because I wanted to remember the mundane yet majestic moment. I wanted to remember because I knew they weren't going to be this little very long. I wanted to remember because I realized the importance of parenting when my daughter wants to be like me. And I knew then – and in so many times since – I'm meant to be their mom.

I wanted to remember those days – even the hard ones. This is my story, and my favorite chapters were just unfolding.

––––––––

When Ben was two, I read some chapters from *Wild Things: The Art of Nurturing Boys* by Stephen James and David S. Thomas. Ben's always ready for an adventure, so I figured I should equip myself for the ride. The authors call 2- to 4-year-old boys "Explorers" and describe them like this:

––––––––––––––––––––

[7] Lucado, Max. The Applause of Heaven: Discover the Secret to a Truly Satisfying Life. Nashville: Thomas Nelson, 1996.

"Explorers are simultaneously delightful and demanding. Their moods swing on a dime, and nothing compares to the joy that overcomes them when they make a new discovery. Boys who are in the Explorer stage are active, aggressive, curious, and self-determined. As strange as it sounds, boys in the Explorer stage demonstrate love and affection through wrestling, head butting, and sometimes even hitting. ... Most of what an Explorer needs from his parents and his caregivers comes in the form of discipline, structure, and patience. For a boy to thrive as an Explorer, he requires boundaries, open space, consistency, and understanding."[8]

I was encouraged that I'm not the first mom who has mothered a boy who sometimes hits his friends, is always moving, can go from frustrated to excited in seconds, and has no fear. Of course, I knew I wasn't alone because I have friends who are raising boys to be great men. But, somehow, hearing a stranger describe my son was comforting.

One day in February 2012, Ben climbed to the top of the netting around a ball pit at a local restaurant with the only decent indoor playground in this town and jumped, shoulder first, into the balls; chewed multiple times on said netting; stole an Andes mint from a neighboring table during the same restaurant outing and put it in his mouth with the paper still wrapping it before I noticed; found a pile of M&Ms from who knows where (probably the floor of restaurant) and then acted like he was gagging when I pulled the chocolaty mess from his mouth; quietly played with some AAA batteries and a vial of insulin that are kept in a zipper pouch in my purse after eating the fruit snacks that are also stored in the pouch in case I have low blood sugar; and bit his sister for the second time in less than a week. And that was just one day.

Some days seem long, but I know I will look back and laugh and be in awe of how far we've come. And, thankfully, not every day is the same.

---

[8] James, Stephen and Thomas, David S. Wild Things: The Art of Nurturing Boys. Carol Stream: Tyndale House Publishers, 2009.

Just like my first-born girl isn't like my second-born son in many ways, moments and days and seasons are their own. Like the adoptions that got us here, mothering is a process. Thankfully, my heavenly Father is used to His kids messing up. The Bible is the only steadfast manual to parenting – or anything else we're called to do in this life.

In the summer of 2012, I spent so much time reading James that I ripped a page of his letter from turning back and forth in my Bible so much. If I did that to my Bible, can you imagine what those words did to my heart?

Consider trials joy. Persevere. Be slow to anger. Be quick to listen. Be slow to become angry. Do what the word of God says. Don't show favoritism. Show mercy. What is faith without deeds? Tame my tongue because where it goes, the rest of me goes. Be wise, and wise people are peacemakers. Draw near to God. Be humble. Realize we're not in control. Be patient.

James reminds me (and that's putting it nicely!) that God wants me to live out my faith with my hands and my feet and my words and my actions and my attitudes and my relationships and my decisions and my whole entire life.

Believe it and then do it – every day, regardless of what circumstances come my way.

Sometimes my pride sneaks in and I boast in my own mind that I found peace when I surrendered biologically producing children and was given these amazing adoption stories. But then real life slaps me in the face again.

That summer I tried to focus on letting God change my heart while I did laundry, made dinner, supported my husband, trained my kids, played with my kids, lived in community with my friends, ran errands, and cleaned my house. I felt like I was on the brink of changing, but then right as I took a step forward, I stumbled backward. I let my frustrations with Greg come out as harsh words. I let my frustrations with my kids come out in a tone I want to take back. I spoke my opinions too quickly. I set my expectations too high, again.

Yet I kept reading James and thinking about how these truths he wrote apply to my life. Life with God as my foundation was the only way to live. I knew I'd be better off for it – and so would the people around me.

Mothering is pleasure and work – often in the same moment. Thankfully, just when I was ready to cry out my inadequacies and failures, I was reminded one day that summer this work isn't meaningless.

Life is a process, like the adoptions.

James talks about perfection, not in our please-everyone, clean-everything, always-succeed way, but rather perfection as a process to be made mature and complete by God's standards. We are to live out our faith despite our circumstances and because of our imperfections. I'm not perfect, but I'm being perfected by a perfect God. Notice the drastic difference when "perfect" is an unattainable adjective and when it's an ongoing verb.

I was being reminded to believe it and live it when Ben, right between being two and three at the time, accidentally locked himself in his bedroom just before I needed to walk out of the house to get to the Bible study on James on time. Then when I made it to the van with both my kids, I realized Ben has put his shoes on himself. Hooray for independence!

I needed that same faith God is perfecting us when I exchanged high fives with the same boy because he peed in the potty for the first time, because as soon as he stepped away from the toilet he peed larger amounts all over the rug. My same sweet boy squeezed a nearly full tube of expensive scar reduction cream all over his legs. Granted, his left thigh was one of the places that needed said cream. Still, the excessive one-time application wasn't what I intended. I shouldn't even try to erase the scars anyway.

James' hard truths mattered to me when plans changed and when loved ones disappointed and when strangers didn't move fast enough and when milk spilled and when I was ready for a new day.

———

I watched the movie *What to Expect When You're Expecting* years ago and it's still a movie I think back on and literally laugh out loud. Starting a family, as with so many other things in life, is never what you expect.

As with our story, sometimes the least expected is even better. These adoptions are obviously my greatest example of how not getting what I expected became my greatest blessings. We have friends who have miscarried, waited longer than seemed necessary to finally hold their babies, been surprised with pregnancy, and adopted. These stories make our families who they are.

So, if you've seen the movie, do you remember Jordan? He's the sword- and stick-wielding boy who got stuck in the soccer net, found a dead cat, and fell down concrete stairs while his daddy walked through the park as part of a daddies group. Jordan made me laugh more than anyone in the whole movie because he's just like Ben, who was almost three when I saw it.

If you haven't seen the movie, at least go watch the trailer. You'll see Jordan. Think of Ben. And maybe you'll catch a glimpse of why I think being a boy mom is hard.

Even so, I want to remember. Ben is all boy. He's funny and animated. He keeps me on my toes – and has since the day we brought him home. Yes, like Jordan, he likes to carry sticks.

Through the laughs, I was reminded God had a plan for my boy. Leigh was a single mother to a baby boy when she conceived Ben. The two boys are two weeks shy of being a year apart. Because of her love for them, Leigh knew raising one boy without a father while working was enough. She courageously sought adoption and in that decision gave Ben a dad.

And let me tell you, my boy wants to be like his daddy. And I pray that he clings to that example, trusts God like his daddy, and grows to live intentionally and bravely.

Sometimes it's hard to see beyond the noises and messes, but some of that will pass. He'll become taller and stronger and more confident. He'll find passions and he'll make friends. He'll learn about the world around him and the God our family chooses to serve.

Even as a second-grader, he's quick to hold doors open for strangers and welcome friends into our house. If someone asks him to pray about something, he will – for many nights in a row. He's learning people feel love in different ways. He loves life and helps those around him love it too.

If he becomes patient and kind like his daddy, I'll be a happy momma. If he loves and serves people like his daddy, the world will be a better place. If he chooses what is right like his daddy, his community will be grateful. If he encourages his wife to be a better version of herself like his daddy does me, his family will thrive.

I want Ben to embrace the example of his daddy because there really isn't a better man to want to be like. That kind of lasting influence is one reason I believe God makes families.

In Their Words :: Sarah Frazer

There's so much I could share about adoption. I could share about the healing in our hearts we've experienced in the past two years. Or I could share the amazing way God has answered our prayers. It was unreal how the answers arrived. I could talk about the fear, rejection, and loss surrounding it all. Then there also is the joy, the long-awaited joy, we experienced.

Instead, I want to tell you how adoption has revealed my need to walk in the daily. Before bringing our sweet China-girl home, my life was busy. Busy with children, busy with a husband who had just started his "dream job," busy with homeschooling and ministries at church. I had no time to slow down.

I enjoyed it. Although I was tired, I believed that was a normal way to feel. I was busy, and happy. We stepped into the adoption world at that same pace. I completed paperwork the first day we got it. I waited (not) very patiently for each step. I wasn't so much in a hurry, as I was living my entire life wrapped around one little thing … control. I wanted to control the outcome of everything, even this adoption.

I would have never said I was in control; I knew enough about God to never say that out loud. But I was a control-freak. I wanted my way and my dream. Once we were handed our daughter, in the civil affair's office in Zhengzhou, China, I suddenly felt the shift of reality: I was never in control.

Our daughter's special needs were much worse than we had planned for and she rejected me right away. I'm embarrassed to admit I cried a lot of angry tears the first week. Okay, for the first six months I cried angry tears. God had "abandoned" me, and my life suddenly stopped. I couldn't homeschool how I wanted. I couldn't be involved in church like I wanted. I felt everything in my life just stopped.

I no longer was able to rush around and be busy. I have four children now, one with special needs and adjustment issues. My months and weeks slowed to days. I lived one day at a time. And it only made me sad and angry. I began to resent the daily living, until I read these words from Psalm 46:1: "God is our refuge and strength, an ever-present help in trouble."

The unexpected medical needs, the unexpected rejection, and the hurt and loss I would personally experience took time to overcome. After 18 months of having our girl home, I had a moment of reflection one Sunday afternoon. Although those 18 months had been the hardest I had ever experienced, I knew God was leading me. It wasn't hard because she's difficult. It was hard because God had a big work to do in my heart, changing my expectations.

The days are still hard, especially Sundays. With the hustle and bustle of the nursery, my little girl just can't handle any small change. On a normal day she is good. But I've learned to just expect the crying, screaming, and tears on Sundays. Sometimes changing my expectations changes everything – especially my response.

And so I've found small nuggets of joy, healing, and peace in walking one day at a time. It takes a lot of faith, and an intense amount of effort to slow down and enjoy the present. I'm still learning. The biggest reason I have been able to walk daily (and enjoy it!) has been because of God's Word. It was the rock we leaned on during the times of the storm. So, I encourage you to find peace and hope and joy in the pages of Scripture.

Sarah Frazer is a writer and mom who invites women to study God's word in their ordinary days at www.sarahefrazer.com.

In Their Words :: Lynsey Day

Long after we'd brought Parker home, I realized that during those first few months with my new son I experienced adoption depression. At a retreat for adoptive moms, I learned I wasn't alone in this initial experience when those first few months of having a baby I had longed for weren't what I thought they would be.

Yes, I loved Parker from that the moment he was put in my arms, but we didn't experience an immediate attachment.

Reflecting on my early days of motherhood, I now see things in a new light. One of those things is the way I treated others. I feared all these people holding my baby may have a better attachment to my son than I did. I remember it bothering me when people held my baby, especially when I was out and about. I remember not exactly being able to put my finger on why it bothered me but it did.

I remember those first months when Parker cried, I cried. He was a colicky baby and those days were hard. As much as I loved him, I felt like I couldn't soothe him like a mom should. I didn't feel like he needed me. I remember crying (a lot) and thinking, "This is all I've wanted for four years and now that I have him, it's horrible!" I remember wanting to keep these thoughts secret. So I kept it in, pushed people away, and pretended like I had everything under control. After much prayer, my sweet angel stopped crying so often and began to recognize my voice, which helped ease my confused heart.

Around four months old, Parker seemed more like mine. We began to really bond and we began to learn each other. Even looking back on the hard days, I wouldn't trade my experience for anything. It's made me stronger and even happier we chose adoption and that God chose Parker for us.

No one tells you about the attachment part. No one warns you it may be a while before he feels like "yours." I wish I had known then what I know now after spending some time with other adoptive moms. I would have been more prepared and possibly saved a few relationships that were damaged by my emotions.

As embarrassing as it is, I feel that there may be some out there who have experienced this or may in the future. If telling my story helps someone else, then it's worth it. My Jesus is a loving and forgiving God and even when we don't deserve it, His mercies are new every morning.

Lynsey Day is a wife, mom of two boys, and follower of Christ who blogs at www.prayuntillsomethinghappens.blogspot.com about infertility, surrogacy, miscarriage, and adoption.

How God Trades Our Sorrow

When life gets really difficult, don't jump to the conclusion that God isn't on the job. Instead, be glad that you are in the very thick of what Christ experienced. This is a spiritual refining process, with glory just around the corner.

(1 Peter 4:12-13, The Message)

Greg and I are both the oldest of three kids, so that has long seemed like a "normal" number of kids to us, although the part of me that likes order has been drawn to the idea of an even number of kids. Ben has the personality of a middle child, so that's where I've always assumed he'd be. Regardless of what we discuss in terms of family planning, though, we really do know we aren't the ones in charge of the plan.

In January 2012, I decided I was ready to adopt again.

Of course, it wasn't that simple.

With the new year came starting fresh. I had been thinking about how to give better, love better, and mother better. You know, all those resolution generalities. But there was more brewing in my heart so I asked God to take away my fear and hesitations and give me fresh perspective while I was driving on a road trip. (If it's not while driving, the best thoughts come to me in the shower.)

During the drive, God opened my heart to the possibility of a third child. It was a big step because I was scared. Going from one by-the-book baby who was potty-trained at two-and-a-half years to two kids was hard. The helplessness passed, mostly. If there's anyone who can explain how an adventurous boy's mind works, I'd listen intently!

In January 2012, I laid it out there – you know, on my blog, on Facebook, and in conversations – that Greg and I were beginning a third adoption process. We brought our two previous adoption experiences to the table, knowing very well a third may not look anything like the previous ones. But we trusted God, who had proven over and over again He was faithful in the details and the sustainer of peace.

Plenty of days in February 2012 were spent working on the stack of paperwork to update our home study. It's only good for a year, so in April 2013 I filled out more paperwork to update it – again. During those two years, we heard about situations through an attorney we hoped to work with and other acquaintances, but nothing ever amounted to more than Greg and I saying, "Yeah, we're interested."

––––––––

Real life doesn't stop for adoption processes.

One June 2013 afternoon in real life, I went missing for about eighteen minutes. Thing is, I didn't know I was missing.

It was one of those days where I had commitments and appointments and responsibilities and plans back to back to back to back. My calendar was already full without all the last-minute additions that happened. Such weeks can be exciting, but they can also create weariness in my momma brain.

That summer day, Cate had been to robotics camp and Ben had been at vacation Bible school. We ended up at lunch with some friends after swapping kids who needed to be transported at different times and from different places.

After lunch we went home and I prepared dinner for a friend whose daughter was recovering from surgery while the kids played/rested/napped. I doubled it, actually, so my family could eat the same thing the following night. King Ranch Chicken Casserole, Spanish rice, brownies and salad were all ready to go.

I had a small window of time between that and needing to be back home to meet my husband so we could go to get our fingerprints done at a particular location forty-five minutes away with a certain FBI-approved machine, the only one in western Kentucky, for one of the few remaining documents required for our home study.

We pulled into my friend's driveway and I left the van running and told the kids to wait in their seats and stay buckled while I took in the food. Now, I should tell you, this friend and I aren't close. We have a mutual friend, really, but I like chatting with her. I hadn't seen her in a while, so we chatted and chatted. Okay, so, we chatted longer than I planned, so long that my kids got unbuckled (So much for obedience! Of course, I hadn't really done the quick drop-off like I planned either!) and came in. Apparently one had to use the bathroom and the other was just along for the social outing. They ended up swinging on a cool swing in the backyard while I finished talking.

I glanced at the time and realized we needed to go. So I rounded up the troops, well, my two kids who are so social they're sometimes more like herding cats. Finally, we all made it back to the van.

My phone buzzed with a new text. I glanced down and realized I had five missed calls and a "Where r u?" text from my husband, who doesn't rely on texting like I do, as well as texts from three friends. I called my husband back. I knew I was cutting it close on time, but I still had seven minutes to make it home. (We live in a small town, you know.) Turns out, he thought we were leaving for our fingerprinting appointment at 3 o'clock that afternoon. I thought we were leaving at 3:15. Greg had contacted at least three of my best friends to see if they knew where I was.

Ah, yes, a miscommunication that, according to the emails I later consulted, was my fault. And, yes, I'm the organized one who planned our departure time. It had been one of those days. It was only Tuesday, but it was one of those weeks. And my brain was scattered and weary. Once again, I tried to fit too much into my day.

Can I confess something, though? I felt loved to know if I went missing, the search party would start after less than 20 minutes. I don't often struggle to feel loved, but it was an out-of-the-blue affirmation that

I'm surrounded by family and friends who care about my well-being. And they (well, at least the one I'm married to ...) apparently also care about my current location and estimated time of arrival.

I pulled in the driveway, picked up my husband who was waiting for me on the front porch, and started our detoured (thanks to construction!) trek to our fingerprinting appointments. Greg's appointment was at 4:10 and mine was at 4:20. We pulled into the parking lot at 4:11 and walked out of the little ink/mail shop about ten minutes later, fingerprinted appropriately for the possible expansion of our family.

Despite the chaos of the day, my heart was full, some friends were blessed with food they didn't have to make, and our home study was one step closer to being finished. And yet again love overshadowed the crowded calendar.

————

As I look back on the summer of 2013, the sequences of events and emotions are a blur.

In June 2013, I talked with an adoption agency director we'll call Nicole who seemed to be the perfect fit for us. A go-getter who was bluntly honest, I liked Nicole immediately and the subsequent emails, texts, and phone calls confirmed that. Before we were officially clients, she asked me about bringing home a baby boy from Nevada, but our home study wasn't updated yet and it wasn't even actually the kind of home study the agency would need. If we'd had the right paperwork, we would have been on a plane later that week.

We spent four days researching the possibility of adopting a two-year-old girl from Bulgaria. She had a name and I had a picture of her sweet, chubby face on my phone. So many variables made the situation something we wanted to pursue, but she had some medical concerns that would likely require regular doctor's appointments and educational resources we don't have in our small town. Not long after we decided not to pursue this adoption, I texted some of my closest friends who knew about this girl and told them about our decision – and that I was sad.

I didn't expect the sadness, especially with the peace I had. My friend Holly who had taken my place in the newsroom offered wisdom that had nothing to do with journalism: It was okay for sadness and peace could co-exist, like rain on a sunny day.

One Sunday that June, I took the weight of my dreams, circumstances, ideas, responsibilities, and emotions that were on my shoulders into church. As we sang a song I'd heard many times before, the words seeped into my heart in a new way:

> "I'm pressed but not crushed, persecuted not abandoned / Struck down but not destroyed /I'm blessed beyond the curse for his promise will endure / And his joy's gonna be my strength"[9]

I was reminded I don't have to carry it on my shoulders. In fact, freedom is found in letting go, in laying it all down.

Father's Day was near. Facebook was exploding with tributes. I'm incredibly thankful for my husband who is an amazing dad to our kids. He's present and involved. He makes me a better mom by loving me well. He makes our family stronger with his leadership. And I couldn't do this life without him – especially when weariness weighs me down.

But even as great as Greg is, we aren't alone in this adoption process or anything else in life. Our heavenly Father has adopted us and promises that everything will work together for the good of those who love Him and have been called according to His purpose (Romans 8:28). It may not seem good now. Pain and hard decisions may be present. But there is more. Glory is just around the corner.

More paperwork was also around the corner.

---

[9] Evans, Darrell. Trading My Sorrows (Yes Lord). Vertical Music, 1998.

I spent July updating paperwork – some of which is just time-consuming because birth certificates, marriage license, adoption decrees, family history, and prior residences don't change. By the end of the month, we had a meeting with Hannah, the social worker who would get our home study officially updated for the agency we wanted to use.

A couple weeks later, Nicole from the agency called me about a homeless fourteen-month-old boy in Jackson, Mississippi. We weren't officially agency clients yet, but she was eager to help us anyway and knew we were getting our home study updated for her. In less than twenty-four hours, we went from thinking we were heading to Mississippi to bring home a boy who needed shelter, food, and a family to hearing the news his homeless mother decided she could manage to take care of him. I'm all about moms trying to mother their own babies, but when a woman can't take care of herself, doesn't have a house, lives in her car, and can't afford her baby's immunizations, sustaining a second life seems quite hopeless.

We used the scenario to push us forward to actually becoming agency clients and scheduled our teleconference interview. This phone conversation was presented to me as a formality. This agency had already tried to help us bring two babies home in the past couple of months. So Greg and I sat on our bed with my cell phone on speaker and answered routine questions from the social worker who was no more than a name to us.

When we talked about interracial adoptions, I felt judged for being a white family living in a small town. Yes, we were open to bringing home a baby who looked different than us. Yes, we'd want the child to know about his cultural heritage. Yes, we have a couple of black friends and go to a small church that values diversity and includes kids adopted from Liberia, China, and Nepal. Yes, we believe in community, which expands resources and opportunities.

When we talked about discipline, I felt like this social worker thought we were the worst mom and dad ever because we don't parent like she does. I left the conversation in tears – the kind of tears that wouldn't stop falling and prevented me from finishing sentences.

I felt defeated, judged, and weary.

The next morning in a follow-up call with Nicole, who wasn't part of the previous night's call, I realized Hannah had misrepresented us in our home study when she updated it. I have no idea why and to this day have never gotten a straight answer as to why she included what she did and left out what she did. Not only were we caught off guard during the interview, but the social worker from the agency was surprised because our home study didn't reflect us. A web of miscommunication and assumption weaved itself around our family.

I needed my people – the ones who know me, who sit around my table for dinner, and who have kids who are my kids' friends. This third adoption process was the most emotional one yet. I felt like I did during those wearisome years of infertility. In fact, I hesitate to even call it a process because that implies movement.

My best friends walked and talked me through the hurts and judgments from the agency rejection. Jaclyn texted me scripture in the middle of her work day. Sarah showed up with muffins and Diet Dr Pepper on a morning I had cried my eyes out – and not eaten breakfast. Courtney, who was recovering from major surgery, prayed for me and checked on me. Our families asked us what we needed them to do.

I emailed some other friends a plea for prayers because I felt trapped by the judgments and frustrations. I was a little worried when I hit send that my friends would ignore my ramblings or perhaps even judge me more than the stranger already had. Most of these people I emailed had been in my house. We'd watched each other's kids. We'd loved and disciplined and laughed and cried and broken down and built up and dreamed together. A couple people are online friends who have been on a God-sized dream journey with me and I figured the extra prayers wouldn't hurt.

I shouldn't have been surprised when I got texts, emails, and phone calls saying: I love you. I love your family. The fact you care what kind of mom you are makes you a good mom. You are not alone. What do you need?

Hebrews 10:24-25 ran through my mind: "And let us consider how we may spur one another on toward love and good deeds, not giving up meeting together, as some are in the habit of doing, but encouraging one another —and all the more as you see the Day approaching."

My friends held me up. They continued to spur me on. They continued to pray. They heard my rambled, cluttered emotions. The real conversations and the hard questions gave me life. Greg and I still hoped to expand our family through adoption. We hoped to bring a child right into our community that truly knows how to love.

————

In the coming months, we gathered ourselves. We talked with our attorney to brainstorm next steps. And we settled on meeting with a different adoption agency a little closer to home.

After two independent adoption processes in 2007 and 2009, we've never loved the idea of adoption agencies. But after waiting a while this time around, we decided that was the route we should take. We met with a second adoption agency the Friday before Christmas 2013. I had reservations but was also excited to see if the new agency would work for us. After a girl in Bulgaria and a homeless toddler didn't work out, I really wanted this agency to be where we were supposed to be. I hoped for a different connection this time.

But after three hours of sitting across a desk from the well-meaning director, I left knowing it wasn't a good fit. On the way to pick up our kids from my mom, I talked to Greg a little but mostly cried.

There wasn't much to say. We knew it was time to let go.

The rest of that evening was filled with sweet distractions courtesy of long-time friends and their families. It was good to laugh about motherhood and memories. It was freeing to say I didn't know what was next. Katie and Bekah have known me since before we could drive, long before I ever thought I'd be a mom. We've giggled about high school crushes, helped each other mend broken hearts, and wondered what it would be like to be adults. Yet our grown-up selves and families continued connecting — albeit not as much as we'd prefer. They were just what I needed that night.

And then the next day came more fellowship that had nothing to do with the desired adoption and everything to do with life. When Greg and I got into bed that night, we finally found the words. Our words were in sync.

We independently arrived at the same decision: We weren't going to pursue anything else adoption-related. And let me tell you, there is so much assurance when God plants two hearts at the same place before we even open our mouths to discuss it. I needed the clarity and peace it brought.

My life has taught me never to say never, so I didn't theorize about our future. We just knew the agency wasn't for us and we needed to let go and lay it all down.

I know we serve a God who gives every good gift in the time that is perfect. And He's good even when I don't get my way. Sometimes letting go makes way for the God-sized dreams He has for us. As I learned, being drawn to Him is the ultimate dream anyway.

We were a family with two healthy, funny kids who fit perfectly with us. Greg and I agreed we didn't yearn for someone who is missing, but we believed we had more to give. Perhaps our family was complete. And we decided to be okay with that.

I also knew I wasn't who I once was. Being a mom has changed me. How I became a mom has changed me. Like those nearly two years of infertility, the more recent two years of pursuing a third adoption have changed me. God drew me to Him and made me think about family and loving the least of these from an eternal perspective.

Perhaps the process that has yet to lead to a third child really was important in ways that truly changed — and will continue to change — my family. Letting go is freeing. Yes, sometimes it feels more like that time Greg and I tandem bungy jumped off a bridge 141 feet above a river in Queenstown, New Zealand. But God's got us, even more securely than those bungy cords had us dangling above a river in 2009.

No matter how many times I hold onto life too tightly, God gives me grace and I loosen my grip. It's not by trying harder or accomplishing more that I'm saved. Only God's grace does that.

> "For it is by grace you have been saved, through faith — and this is not from yourselves, it is the gift of God — not by works, so that no one can boast. For we are God's handiwork, created in Christ Jesus to do good works, which God prepared in advance for us to do" (Ephesians 2:8-10).

Life is a process, even when we don't see exactly what God has prepared for us.

In laying down the adoption process, I felt free to live my life, the one right now, right here, that doesn't involve a script. Because I'm not really in control anyway. Because I have two kids who need more than a distracted momma wishing for more. Because my husband and I were unified in our decision — about this one thing and so many other things.

And, you know, just like that time I stopped trying to become pregnant, I had peace.

———

Not much more than a month after we laid down our adoption pursuit, an attorney friend told his incarcerated, pregnant client Heather about us when she mentioned she may be interested in making an adoption plan. Once again, we were interested, especially after Greg had a conversation with Heather's mom in February 2014.

Yes, I admit, part of me wondered if God was blessing our obedience to let go by finally providing an open door to what we really wanted. While God was certainly capable of doing that, getting our way wasn't guaranteed in exchange for our obedience and faithfulness.

A possible shock probation, impending drug rehab, and older children in the care of their father who was not the baby's father all surely played a role in Heather's decision. But we had to wait – yes, some more – to find out whether she would parent or make an adoption plan.

In March, Heather's mom called Greg again to check in and ask some more questions about adoption in general. We considered it a good sign we were still on her radar. Honestly, I was relieved that for the first time Greg was on the receiving end of the information. My instinct is to be involved and gather information, but this time I had to hear secondhand as it unfolded. Of course, I still asked my husband plenty of questions. I have no doubt God knew this was best for me emotionally and planned accordingly.

"She's pregnant with twins!" was news Heather's mom shared with Greg during another phone conversation in April. We've long been intrigued with the idea of twins, so our excitement grew.

In May, Heather gave birth to a baby boy and baby girl – news Greg received in another phone call from Heather's mom. She chose names for them, but we still weren't sure of her parenting plan. Because she returned to jail after recovering from her C-section, her mom was given power of attorney over two tiny babies in a NICU in Louisville, Kentucky.

When Greg hung up the phone, we immediately went into hypothetical planning mode.

What if she chose us to parent these little babies? The NICU was in the same city where my mom lives, making logistics more convenient.

Our kids were getting ready to finish the school year so our family calendar was fairly free and could be totally clear with a few moments' notice. We had an extended family vacation to Hilton Head Island, South Carolina., planned about a month later that we would abandon if we could parent these babies.

Early in Ben's life, I've had him pegged as a middle child. As he became aware we'd like to adopt another baby, Ben often said we should bring home two at once – a girl who could share Cate's bedroom and a boy who could sleep in his old bedroom, the one that was once a nursery but had been converted into a guest room for my emotional well-being.

During the spring of 2014, I wondered many times if these babies were what God had planned for our family, even knowing I had no idea what I was getting into with twins. One baby alone would rock our stroller- and diaper-free life, but I still knew I'd care for them in an instant if given the chance.

Other than one text, Greg never heard from Heather's mom again. Last we knew, Heather had completed the drug rehab program and the babies were with her mom. Whether that's the long-term plan is unknown to us, but I still think about the babies sometimes and wonder.

We were disappointed, again, but we believe God is the maker of families and will forever cling to our faith, which Hebrews 11:1-3 describes: "Now faith is confidence in what we hope for and assurance about what we do not see. This is what the ancients were commended for. By faith we understand that the universe was formed at God's command, so that what is seen was not made out of what was visible."

———

When I was a kid, I used to love rearranging my bedroom furniture. Somehow I would manage to move the full-sized canopy bed, dresser, and bookshelf/drawer combo around the dark brown carpet all on my own. I'd avoid blocking the three windows that overlooked our backyard and the neighbor's yard that diagonally separated my yard from my friend's.

Even then, I liked order. For someone who has long been reluctant to embrace change, I have no idea why rearranging my bedroom furniture was appealing. Perhaps controlling the change was comfortable for my perfectionist ways.

I could fall asleep soundly with my bed in a different place, but anticipating a change in life I don't have control over could keep me up at night.

Yet when we follow Jesus, we have to rearrange our lives.

I heard that in a sermon in church one Sunday in February 2014 and I was taken back to pushing and pulling my furniture across the carpet.

I remember how I've dug in my heels so many times. I've stalled changes in life because I was afraid of what the new season would bring. I've resisted change because I wasn't in control of what would happen next. I've said never to living where I live, accepting a job I didn't think I wanted, quitting said job to be a stay-at-home mom, and enrolling my kids in a private school that turned out to be a perfect fit for us.

Never say never, I know.

Because Jesus may call me to lay down something or pick up something new or invite someone in or go against what I've always known or take steps into the unknown. God doesn't leave us the same. He makes us new and continues making us new. He doesn't leave us in the wilderness but changes us as we journey to the Promised Land.

Since I let go of pursuing a third adoption, I'd paused by that room I thought we'd make a nursery. It's been sitting there. Empty. Bare. It's right across from my bedroom, next to our bathroom, just off the dining room, so I would see it many times a day.

God laid on my heart the desire to give the room purpose again, so I converted it into a guest room in February 2014. I had no idea if it would forever be a guest room, but this rearranging was necessary for my soul as I followed Jesus. Moving around furniture that time wasn't as easy as when I was a kid, but I'm glad I did it.

In the process of life, God rearranges our desires and our decisions. He fills our hearts with convictions we never anticipated being important. He perfects us through real life that often looks nothing like we imagined. Sometimes it's hard, but we're always better for it.

I don't want to be scared to let go. Rather, I want peace that takes me back to resting peacefully in that childhood canopy bed of mine wherever it was in my bedroom. I want to rest in what Jesus has for me, even when it means rearranging my thoughts, desires, dreams, and expectations. These sorts of changes bring peace because the One who leads me doesn't change.

God is faithful in all things – including hearing the desires of our hearts – because we are his children, adopted into a true forever family.

In Their Words :: Kim Crouch

My husband Stephen and I began traveling to Guatemala in 2009 to do mission work. On that first trip, we met so many orphans and it was clear adoption was in our future. We had no idea when; we just knew God had placed it on our hearts to pursue adoption at some point.

It's been a long journey with many tears and lots of prayer, pleading with God for just one more baby. Eleven years ago, our first child came without trying. When he was a year old, we were ready for another. After what seemed like a long year of infertility struggles, I turned to taking several different fertility medications throughout the coming years. Most of them made me cuss like a sailor, completely crazy (or should I say crazier), not to mention experiencing hot flashes, and frequent irrational episodes of projecting my infertility-induced anger onto Stephen. It was too much. I quit taking the pills and four months later, we conceived on our own. Now we had brothers almost three-and-a-half years apart.

The depression that came alongside the infertility struggles has been seasonal for me. There have been entire months at a time where I'm fine. Others where it's all I thought about and felt so dark and hopeless, barely clinging to God's word and His promises wondering if He even heard my prayers.

In December 2015, we experienced one of the worst tragedies we've ever been through when our dear friend's child who meant so much to us died in her sleep at just three years old. While sitting in a pew, listening to her parents present her eulogy, God spoke clearly to us on His plans for growing our family. It was the first time I've felt at total peace during this infertility season.

We began the adoption process shortly after and I went on birth control for the first time in our thirteen-year marriage. Choosing to take birth control was one of the most freeing, most certain moments I've had during this process, convinced that I was okay with not conceiving again. It was a moment of relief to finally exhale and let go of "trying."

In January 2016, we contacted CCAI Adoption Services, the same agency our friends had used to adopt their daughter we were mourning. We felt very strongly that God wanted us to use this agency and the same special needs program.

The infertility, all the sadness and doubt, the death of our friends' daughter ... when I look back on all of it, a lump still forms in my throat and my eyes fill up with tears all over again. It reminds me of a verse in one of my favorite songs "Blessings" by Laura Story: "And what if trials of this life / The rain, the storms, the hardest nights / Are Your mercies in disguise?"

Because you see, if we had conceived a third baby on our own, we would have missed out on one of the greatest blessings in our lifetime. He reminded me again to trust in His perfect plan. On April 6, 2016, we received the call we had been matched with a baby girl we named Millie Joy.

Millie Joy came home in January 2017. Kim Crouch loves Jesus, her family, her skincare consultant job, missions, fashion, and any peanut butter and chocolate combo — and she blogs about it all at www.crouchcrew.com.

In Their Words :: Monica Bidwell

Upon beginning the adoption process in 2008, my husband Scott and I heard many adoptive parents say, "Adoption is not for the faint of heart." It seemed to be the mantra of the whole process. Looking back, it almost seems to be an understatement.

Like so many others, our adoption stories were filled with trials, long periods of waiting, and lots of paperwork. Bringing home our two boys was a larger-than-life endeavor. But, as believers in Christ, it became clear to us we were not simply up against the difficulties of the adoption procedure. There was more going on. We were becoming keenly aware we were in a battle – not a battle against the waiting, the frustrations, and the paperwork snafus, but specifically against the spiritual forces of darkness in the heavenly places (Ephesians 6:12).

When believers in Christ decide to adopt a child, it is essentially a declaration of war against Satan himself because adoption is a picture of the gospel. Adoption speaks to who God is and what He has done to redeem His people. The gospel proclaims we were once far-off, unable to save ourselves and spiritually fatherless, but God adopted us into His family through Christ. We, like helpless orphans, could not choose Him. He chose us first. In His perfect love, He grafted us into His family. As believers in Christ, when Scott and I chose to adopt, we not only desired to grow our family, we longed to raise a child in the instruction and love of the Lord. Is it any wonder that Satan would desire to place obstacles in the way of this endeavor?

Because we were already parents when we began the adoption process, we were well aware that bringing a child into your lives was no easy feat. In the pursuit of having our biological daughter, we had experienced the heartache and grief of two miscarriages. Fast-forward to the pursuit of our boys, and our adoption processes included disheartening miscommunications, two traumatic disruptions in which birthmothers changed their minds, and the loss of thousands of dollars (much of which was donated by our family and church friends specifically for our adoptions).

In the weeks and months following the adoption disruptions, we would often ask the Lord, "Didn't you want us to adopt?" "Why does the process seem to go so smoothly for some of the unbelieving families around us while our process is so messed up?" "God, can't you just intervene and have them sign the documents so we can sleep at night?" "Why does every little thing about adoption have to be so hard?" When we would raise these questions, it seemed God would continually remind us of our own spiritual adoption in Him.

His adoption of us is no small thing. There were no mounting adoption fees for Him to pay, no extensive mounds of paperwork. The price was infinitely higher. The blood of His Son, the perfect sacrifice to satisfy His wrath, was the cost of bringing us into His family.

To participate in an earthly adoption of a child into our family was to picture something holy and it would be a fight to the finish. As we labored for our boys, we grew in our relationship with our Heavenly Father. God was not only interested in bringing children into our home, He was changing us and molding us into His image. To Him be all the glory for allowing us to persevere through battle and finish the journey we started to adopt our boys. To Him be all the glory for finishing the process of adopting us!

Monica Bidwell is a Christ follower, wife and mom to three who enjoys being an adoption advocate as she serves in camp ministry alongside her husband Scott.

How God Gives Life

This is what the Lord says — your Redeemer, who formed you in the womb: I am the Lord, the Maker of all things, who stretches out the heavens, who spreads out the earth by myself ...

(Isaiah 44:24)

One morning in January 2013, I was almost ready for church when I heard my kids – who were five and three – picking on each other. The arguments diffused as quickly as they started, and then I noticed a little chair pulled up close to the kitchen counter. The evidence that Ben had reached permanent markers he wasn't supposed to reach irritated me. He walked toward me talking about wanting to color and I noticed him sticking the eraser end of a pencil in his ear.

My irritation rose, but I tried to hide it.

"Ben, you aren't even using the markers correctly. Put 'em up! Find a book to bring with you to church." I should have learned barking orders, especially more than one order, is fruitless.

"The book doesn't go in your mouth, Ben!"

"Why can't you just obey?!" I yelled, again.

Greg tried to tell me to chill out. Of course, that annoyed me, too. I angrily picked up some toys I thought my son should have already taken back to his room. I knew in that emotional moment I should have showed more grace, spoken softer, loved more, moved more slowly, and remembered kids will be imperfect kids. My imperfections were shining through oh-so brightly, yet I was expecting perfection from my boy who still depends on me so much for guidance.

Meanwhile, it was time to leave for church so I started corralling my people in the minivan. As I was doing so, I realized it was much colder outside than I thought, requiring me to backtrack to get Cate's coat as Greg helped Ben with his. I flung open the door and heard the door knock into something. Something was actually someone. The door knob hit Ben's head right above his ear.

I felt terrible.

Moments earlier, I had been chewing him out in such a nagging way. Admittedly, I was still irritated with having to remind and repeat and corral and correct. Yet none of that had anything to do with my poor timing of opening the door and Ben's unfortunate location in the path of the door knob. All of my woe-is-me-as-a-mom emotions were pushed aside by my wanting to comfort Ben, who didn't cry as much as I thought he would normally and was barely talking, which was strange for my boy who sings and growls and talks nearly constantly.

Ben seemed shocked, sad, and mad. He didn't want to talk to me. He wanted Daddy. On the way to church, I finally got a response when I asked him to growl like a dinosaur. It was strange but sweet music to my ears – and heart, which was so heavy. I told Ben I was sorry for yelling at him. He gave me a kiss as Daddy held him as we sang songs to open the church service.

But God wasn't done with my heart.

Our pastor mentioned Sanctity of Life Sunday, a time set aside to bring awareness to how many lives have been lost through abortion. January 2013 was the fortieth anniversary of Roe v. Wade. Since that decision legalized abortion, at least 55,808,387 babies weren't given a chance to live, according to information provided by our local crisis pregnancy center.

That's 55.8 million stories that remain untold.

God still wasn't done speaking to my heart.

That same Sunday, my friend Corrie gave an update about her high-risk pregnancy and her baby girl who was not developing properly in the womb. There was the possibility Lucy Pearl may not breathe for long outside the womb. Best-case scenario was dwarfism. (Lucy lives and breathes. Her limbs are shorter than normal, but she's a happy, healthy girl.)

A prayer time for my friend and her unborn baby followed. I was so encouraged by my friend's faith in God and belief God is indeed good all of the time, even when the world as we want it comes crashing down. I prayed for that same peace that passes all understanding that held me together so many times before to cover Corrie and her family.

I wanted to take back yelling and nagging at Ben earlier that morning and, unfortunately, other times since. I walked back to my seat in the church sanctuary feeling grateful. Mandy and Leigh chose life for my kids. They cared for them and delivered them with such bravery and grace. I was thankful in that moment for Greg, who loves me so much he wants me to trust God and give Him control over every detail in my life, especially my words. I was thankful for a faith community that prays and encourages one another in real life.

God perfects me and refines me and strengthens me through my imperfections. That's what He was doing then and what He continues to do.

Not long after that, I realized all those ways God spoke to my heart that Sunday morning come down to this: I'm pro-life. I would have told you I was pro-life long before I knew adoption was going to be my family's story. But then I adopted twice and my definition of pro-life changed.

Since bringing Cate and Ben home, I've realized pro-life is more than a political stance. It's also a belief children are a blessing and not a burden. I'm so grateful my kids' birth moms recognized this, too. We're raising our kids among a community of friends who believe this, too.

When we moms stand together, support each other, and commit to doing our best for our kids and the ones around us, then we're pro-life. When we help our friends who are welcoming foster children into their homes, those gifts of money and clothing say we're pro-life. We discipline and teach and train and advise and shepherd and guide and entertain these children we love. We plan for their futures because we believe they deserve futures.

Through our adoptions, God demonstrated He is continually near. He's in the details. And He's faithful to hear the desires of our hearts. Do you know why? He's pro-life, too. God values life. He wants our lives to bring Him glory and He wants us to raise our kids – the biological ones, the adopted ones, the ones who may be in our homes temporarily – with His eternal kingdom as the foundation.

God values life so much He adopts us into His family.

Just like Greg and I gave Cate and Ben our last name, God calls us His own. Just like we welcomed our kids into the responsibilities and privileges of being in a family, God welcomes us into His home. Yes, there are glimpses of His kingdom here on earth, but there's also a promise of the eternal home Jesus is preparing for us. Because we are God's. Because our names have been changed and our covenants sealed. Because we serve a God who believes in life.

We adopted Cate and Ben. They're our children. They're named in our wills. And they didn't have to do anything to be called daughter and son. We chose them in the beginning and we choose them still. We choose life. Thankfully we all are welcomed by our heavenly Father who continues choosing us and calls us His own.

––––––––––

On Election Day 2016, I was reminded even when we see God's faithfulness in our everyday life, we still have to have hard conversations sometimes. Without what we'd be through to become a family, the question my first-grade son was getting ready to ask me may have left me speechless.

"Mom, why do people say Hillary Clinton wants to kill babies?" Ben said as soon as the minivan door slid closed at the bus stop.

I was already grieving an exhausting election and my first-ever vote for a third-party presidential candidate. I felt mellow and defeated, even before learning Donald Trump would become our 45th president. I turned down Big Daddy Weave's "The Lion and the Lamb," which had been on repeat in my head and in my minivan that day.

And I took a deep breath.

I knew one day I would have to explain abortion to my kids, but I wasn't expecting the question to come from Ben, especially in that moment. Cate and Ben buckled their seat belts and I pulled onto the road toward home with tears in my eyes.

I told them some women decide to stop babies' heartbeats because they don't want to be pregnant. They don't want to carry those babies for nine months – even if it meant making an adoption plan like their birth moms did. Abortion means women aren't choosing life for another person.

I told them about how women have to go special doctor offices for a procedure that stops a heartbeat, but how, thankfully, people in Murray, Kentucky, have to go to bigger cities to see that kind of doctor.

And then I told them about how Mandy and Leigh wanted them to have life. They didn't believe they could care for them in all the ways they wanted to. They wanted them to have a mom and a dad. They wanted them to have life.

"So if Leigh didn't find you, would I have died?" That's where Ben's mind went.

"No, she chose life for you and God wanted you to be in our family." That's what I know to be true.

In this first conversation about abortion, my answer was enough. But there is so much more that will have to be discussed and sifted. We will have to talk about how not all unexpected pregnancies result in life. There are gruesome details to what an abortion procedure is and how far into the pregnancy it can be done. We will love people who don't believe life begins at conception like we do. We will see commercials and hear debates in the next election cycle that will overflow into our conversations.

I will tell them again and again their lives matter. I will remind them their birth moms chose to give them life and a family instead of interrupting their heartbeats – that's truth that remains regardless of who is our country's president.

In Their Words :: Melissa Harrell

Hello, my name is Melissa, and I am attached.

I was attached to the newborn foster baby we brought home from the hospital and later to the thirteen-year-old girl who quickly became part of our family. It's really difficult to explain to people who don't feel God's call on their lives to foster why on earth we would jump in to such an undertaking. "I don't know how you do it." "I'd get too attached." "Isn't it going to be so hard to give her back?" "Do you just try to put your guard up?" These are all various questions and concerns I hear regarding foster care. And that's normal!

Everything we are given can be taken away. Scripture is clear about that! In the fall of 2016, we had two biological children, one foster teenager, the baby growing in me, and memories of the foster baby we parented earlier in the year. In reality, I love them equally. And I know that they are all the Lord's and neither are guaranteed to be with me throughout this lifetime. Anyone can be taken away from us at any time! People fail to understand that perspective in the wholeness of their lives and reduce it to solely being a result that can happen from fostering.

When you feel God put a call on your life, you can't ignore it even if you know it might result in some pain. When God sent his Son to this earth, Christ knew He would endure pain. The greatest pain this world has even known. But the eternal reward is far greater. We are not special. Our hearts are not unbreakable. But our faith is. So, we are attached. Oh, so attached. And these children deserve every bit of it.

No matter how your family is formed, parenting is a gift. There's a discouraging stigma attached to fostering and adoption: That you would only do so if you struggle with infertility or if you're "done having your own kids."

Let's be the generation that completely destroys that line of thought. No child, no matter how they are brought into a family, is a back-up plan to pregnancy. Be supportive of however someone decides to blend their family based on what God has called them to do and purposed for their lives. Find your role in that and get involved. That's the difference between being pro-birth and pro-life.

"Religion that God our Father accepts as pure and faultless is this: to look after orphans and widows in their distress and to keep oneself from being polluted by the world" (James 1:27).

If we claim to be a child of God, this verse applies to us. It won't look the same for everybody, but it should look like something for everybody. We will never stop advocating for every believer to search their hearts for what role they are to play in orphan care.

Melissa Harrell is a wife and mom whose calendar is full of her kids' activities, her own stage performances, and her husband's sporting events.

In Their Words :: Kayla Slack

My husband and I experienced two failed matches when we were going through the adoption process. God has certainly redeemed all of this, but I don't want to downplay how brutal these experiences were for us. We were devastated, confused, heartbroken, and very angry. We still trusted and believed that God was in control, but our hearts were shattered.

One of the things that truly hurt me the most about the adoptions falling through was losing the relationship with the birth mothers. We went from talking daily to nothing suddenly. There were no hugs, no goodbyes, and no closure. Just a lot of tears, screaming, and pain.

My husband and I grew very close to both of these birth mothers and cared very deeply for them. We loved them, hurt for them, and we wanted to do everything we could to help them improve their situations. How do you show love to these women once everything has fallen apart for you? How do you continue to love them when you feel so angry? How can you even show love, grace, and forgiveness to them when they just drop out of your life? The answer typically is you can't.

In my opinion, after a birth mother decides to parent it is often easier for her to ignore anything that reminds them the adoption plan they considered. I can understand and even respect that, but my heart just ached to be able to check on them and see how they were doing.

I decided to reach out via text to the first birth mom about a week after she decided to parent. In order for me to move on, I needed her to know we still loved her. I wanted her to experience grace and forgiveness and the only way I had left to show her was with my words. My text read, "Just wanted you to know we still think of you often. It makes me sad that our lives won't be meshed together for the rest of our lives, but we trust in God's plan for our family. Our hope is in the Lord so we are making it. You do not have to respond to this, I just needed to say something for closure for me. We genuinely hope you all are doing well and have such a great life." I received no response to this text, but I prayed God would use it to let her know and feel grace.

Our second birth mom came to us through friends networking locally about three weeks after the first failed match. Although we were scared, we decided we needed to love her. It is hard to put yourself out there emotionally for anyone once you have experienced a failed adoption, but this is one way we can love the least of these as Jesus commands – even when it leads to a second failed adoption.

This second mother decided to parent as well. The difference in this relationship from our first birth mom is that this one continued after the adoption disruption. She reached out to me a few months after her son's birth because she felt desperate and didn't know what else to do.

My heart was broken for her, but I also was so honored she trusted me. I was able to love her for a short while and I even got to meet her son. But then the communication stopped, which saddened me greatly. I know being my friend probably brings up a lot of hard memories for her, and I respect that.

I am still trying to accept the fact we really will never know how long these relationships will last and they may come and go in our lives forever. I only see two choices – to love despite all your fears and insecurities or don't love. If we would have known how either of these relationships would end, I may not have loved like I did. We are called to love because Christ loved us and gave His all for us and so that's what I hope to do. My heart for adoption really has spilled over to love these mommas who feel alone and really just want a friend to be beside them in their hard season of life.

Even though everyone who pursues adoption knows failed matches are a possibility, the broken relationships aren't something for which you can prepare. We only have control over the love we give – even if we don't know how long we'll be in position to do that.

After the heartache and challenges, our adoption process finally ended with a sweet girl born two weeks after our second failed match.

Kayla Slack is crazy about her husband and daughter and loves the patients she sees as a home health nurse like family.

How God Writes More of the Story

My people, hear my teaching; listen to the words of my mouth. I will open my mouth with a parable; I will utter hidden things, things from of old — things we have heard and known, things our ancestors have told us. We will not hide them from their descendants; we will tell the next generation the praiseworthy deeds of the Lord, his power, and the wonders he has done.

(Psalm 78:1-4)

The first-year teacher was discussing the life cycle of a mammal with a dozen first- and second-graders when she drew upon comparison to shield the bulk of the bird and the bees talk: "You know, like you were born from your mom."

My daughter Cate decided to inform her class: "I wasn't in my mom's belly. I'm adopted."

I'm sure she caught her teacher, who was just twenty-two years old, off guard. But that was that.

But the story said more to me. It made me thankful Cate recognizes her birth story is different than most of her friends yet she isn't ashamed to share it. Being adopted is normal for her because we've talked about it since the day she was born. These are the conversations we have regularly, each time revealing more details about her birth mom, our time with this young woman who helped us have a family, and her birth we witnessed.

In 2013, Cate wanted to know more about the seven nights we spent in the hotel waiting for the interstate adoption paperwork to be approved by folks in Indianapolis and Frankfort, Kentucky. I showed her pictures of her birth mom for the first time on her sixth birthday. It was the sweetest, most revealing adoption conversation we had shared up to that point.

This topic is an ongoing dialogue around our house. The word "adoption" has long been in Cate's vocabulary, but we gradually elaborated on the details of her story with her. From the time they were just days old, strangers have told us how much Cate looks like me or Ben resembles my husband's family. Sometimes we grin and nod. Other times we let them in on this story of ours.

My husband and I are raising a girl who remembers details and isn't afraid to tell the truth along with a boy who embraces life to its fullest. We're bringing up two of the best things God has ever done for us. Adoption is the story of how we became a family. It's one I will tell over and over as long as someone listens. And now I'm glad to know my girl will tell it, too.

———

About a month after Cate declared her adoption to her class, she had the chance to meet her birth mom. My six-year-old girl told me later she didn't know how meeting Mandy would be. As her mom, I was so excited about this meeting, even though I wasn't exactly sure how it would go either.

Cate was a little quieter than usual at first, but the more she told her about learning to ride a bike and her school, the more comfortable she became. Before long, she was asking questions and telling stories packed with details as usual.

The circumstances of the day prompted the conversation weeks before between Mandy and me. It was going to be logistically convenient for Cate to meet her. So we talked about it. I told her about how I thought it would be for Cate. She shared what she was comfortable doing.

And we did it. I'm so thankful we did.

Cate actually saw Mandy when she was three months old and she's heard about her since. Just a couple months shy of nineteen when she birthed Cate, Mandy went on to finish college, marry, work as a nurse, and become a mother to twin girls and later a baby boy.

More than six years earlier, Mandy and I had shared so many lunches together before and after doctor's appointments. I'm not sure either of us would have imagined this: We were sharing another meal together and my girl chose to sit next to her birth mom as I sat across from them. And Mandy graciously and bravely got to know the Cate I'm proud to call my daughter.

Yes, Cate was only six, but she was so accepting of adoption right then, which is why I believed it to be a good time for this meeting to happen. I also know how Cate remembers details of events and people. And her birth mom is a person I certainly want her to remember.

Thankfully, Mandy agreed.

"It was a very exciting and somewhat unsettling moment. It was the first time Cate would remember meeting me. My family was very excited for me and I feel like they made a much bigger deal of it than I did. I was excited to get the initial meeting out of the way and get to know her personality a little. She was just like all the pictures that I have seen. She has quite a personality – very talkative and mature. It was a good experience. I was happy that we could meet and start our relationship. I think meeting with her at a younger age was very beneficial to her and her comfort level with being adopted. It will also help her deal with some of the questions that might come up later in life and being comfortable with asking them. It helped me get more comfortable with the idea of answering questions for her. It will only get easier and easier to see her from here out."

I realize this arrangement could be awkward, but it wasn't for us. The time together was surprisingly natural. Yet maybe I shouldn't be surprised because this is what God orchestrated and covered with His peace that passes all my understanding.

Like every child is different, every adoption is different. Birth moms process adoptions differently and want different kinds of relationships throughout the process and in the years that follow. That's okay.

Our story with Ben's birth mom is different but one we also value and hold dear. A younger boy with a different personality, Ben hasn't been in the same place as Cate with adoption. And that's okay too. He knows he's adopted and he'll know more as he's ready to hear it. Adoption isn't a one-conversation topic – these stories are still being written.

So much of adoption is about faith. Faith in God. Faith in the birth moms. Faith in the process. Faith in the conversations that come as the kids grow up. I believe adoption stories matter and I'm grateful Cate has a face to put with such an important name in her story.

––––––––––

Like any adopted child, Cate coming into our family was only the beginning of her story. God has been writing so many other chapters in our girl's life. One of my favorites started Fourth of July weekend in 2015, when Greg, Cate, and I along with ten others from our area left our comfortable surroundings for a week-long mission trip in Chichicastenango, Guatemala.

We took fifty-pound suitcases packed with clothes, school supplies, soccer balls, and toiletries to donate. We carried on our own stuff in smaller suitcases and filled our backpacks with things we thought we needed. But no expectations were packed for my first mission trip.

In the months leading up to the trip, I'd emailed with Katie, who works for Compassion International as a donor relations manager. This trip to Guatemala wasn't a Compassion trip, which is something I'd like to do another time. Katie and I initially connected in December when Greg and I made a donation and she called to thank me. I emailed her again months later when I was trying to make meeting our Compassion-sponsored girl Roselyn, who lives in Guatemala, happen while we're there. Sadly, that wouldn't work out with our mission trip schedule and Compassion's travel guidelines.

But Katie prayed for my family as we experienced a country she loves. And she emailed the week before we left to offer some encouragement. The sincerity in her words was so good for me. To know someone I've never met in person has invested themselves in our trip has reminded me how God's Kingdom works.

Katie put words to my prayers and hopes for this mission trip and for life in general: "When we are able to approach life and the opportunities the Lord gives us with open hands rather than tight-fisted, He fills those anxious places with so much joy and peace in His presence. It is certainly not an accident that you all will be on this trip, and I know He will work in and through you."

Of course, God worked all week.

Our team of thirteen people, plus the four missionaries who live there, divided up most days to serve. We also worked with a local pastor and volunteers who knew how to speak the Quechí dialect many of the local people with Mayan roots spoke. Collectively, we built three houses on concrete slabs, visited sixteen families, and distributed thirty-five wheelchairs. When we visited families, we gave them clothes, shoes, toiletries, and school supplies. We prayed with people and figured out how Bethel could meet other needs, like build a bathroom or secure education and food sponsorships. I may not have understood every word, but I know it was the same Spirit leading people's hearts.

We spent our last day in Guatemala on the black sand beach at Puerto San Jose. The Pacific Ocean waves were mighty, but the men and kids found their way in and out of the white caps. The women snapped many pictures. After a week of serving, we rested in each other and God's beauty.

That afternoon, Cate came to me from where she had been digging in the sand and said, "Mom, can I talk to you?"

I leaned toward her, thinking she was going to tell me about all the sand that had piled up in her bathing suit or ask another question about just how the volcanic ash created a black sand beach. "No, over there," she urged wanting me to step away from our friends.

We walked a few steps away and she says, "I want to be baptized in a few weeks."

My heart melted in that moment. This had been brewing. We'd have conversations many Sundays for months when the communion elements were passed through the congregation. She asked about what accepting Christ and baptism meant. Greg and I have shared our stories over time with her. But, really, it had been a while since we talked about it, even though I'd been praying for her faith journey.

Standing in our bathing suits on the edge of Guatemala, I asked my girl some questions and then called Greg over to join our conversation. Cate repeated to Greg what she had told me. We talked more about sin and separation from God and how Jesus makes eternal life possible. Knowing her personality is so much like mine, I reminded her that even when we choose to live for Jesus, we'll still make mistakes. This life is a process of becoming more like Jesus. But it won't be until we're in heaven that we're made complete and perfect. I hope she grasps this earlier than I did.

God makes us new – and seeing my daughter accept this truth was such a sweet moment, especially after everything we'd seen and experienced together that week. We had a front-row seat to joy and poverty like never before. Really, the whole mission trip reminded me of *Inside Out* and how sadness and joy co-exist.

Earlier in the week, Cate said, "I should trust God more. These people trust God even though they don't have much." To hear her deeper understanding of needing Jesus will forever be a favorite moment in mothering her. Sure, it actually has nothing to do with me and everything to do with God. But I'm grateful that's the kind of God we get to serve together because of adoption.

Cate was adopted a second time – this time by her Heavenly Father – and because of that her earthly father baptized her at our church three weeks after our mission trip to Guatemala. Adoption gave me much – including my oldest girl who is now also my sister in Christ.

In Their Words :: Maria Rosa

I love family traditions and love to see them passed on from one generation to the next. The first thing that comes to mind might be Grandma's recipe or Dad's love of gardening. But in my family, I hope adoption is always a part of our family traditions. As an adoptee myself, I've always known adoption would somehow be woven in to my life.

I was adopted by my parents as an infant and know beyond a shadow of a doubt that's where God always planned for me to be. Adoption has always been such a wonderful and special part of my life that I longed to recreate that experience in my family as an adult. Luckily, my husband shared that desire and we knew early in our marriage that we had the hoped for a large family and hoped and prayed that God's plan included both biological and adopted children for our home.

After being blessed with two precious biological sons, we experienced a season of infertility that we know was certainly God's way of reminding us that He knows best and knew that "now" was the time for us to pursue adoption. Adoption has changed A LOT since the route my parents took thirty-something years ago. There are so many options and paths to adoption, which is both incredibly exciting and also quite a bit overwhelming.

We spent eighteen months researching, reading, discussing, and mostly praying for God to show us the way. We still don't know exactly what our path to adoption will look like but we know God has "our baby" out there somewhere just like He had me for my parents and just like He's adopted us into His family. We hope to hold that baby (or babies) in our arms soon – and maybe someday they will carry on our family traditions.

Maria Rosa shared this in October 2016 as she and her husband were becoming certified as foster parents and have since welcomed a foster baby into their lives.

In Their Words :: Kathleen Guire

Adopting an older child is like reading a novel from the middle instead of the beginning. We parents enter in the middle of the story. The child, or children in my case, have a history. Their history usually has trauma. Child development expert Dr. Karyn Purvis calls referred to them, as "children from hard places."

My children were just that; they didn't have a picture-perfect beginning. They had two years of orphanage living under their belts to boot. When my four adopted children "came home" from Poland to the Guire household in West Virginia, they had nothing to their names, physically, but so much emotional baggage that it barely fit through the doorway. These beautiful, half-written stories entered our household with their survival mode in full swing.

My three biological children were learning the language of grace as my adopted children learned the language of family. It was an interesting dance. Some days it flowed like milk and honey in the Promised Land and other days we seemed to be lost in the wilderness. But we persevered. We laughed and cried together. We fought the demons of their pasts linked arm in arm and often fist to fist.

What does adoption look like later? With sixteen years of our forever family behind us and most of my children grown into adults, I'd say it looks good on the Guires.

My bios have come to me and thanked me for adopting. It has given them a sensitivity to pain in others they would not have had otherwise. When one son took a job in a homeless shelter, he had compassion built in from early life that poured out of him into relationships he formed there. The residents could tell he cared.

My adopted children have thanked me, all but the youngest (give him time). Truth be told, I didn't adopt for a showering of thanksgiving. I did it to build a forever family. However, it is a true sign of maturity and healing my children – all of my children – recognize the gift of adoption. It is the gift of grace offered one day, healing another and daily dying to self. Isn't that what family is?

Kathleen Guire is a mother of seven, writer, teacher, and encourager who blogs at thewholehouse.org.

How God Connects Neighbors

God sets the lonely in families ...

(Psalm 68:6)

More than a year after I let go of the third adoption process, I sat in a house overlooking Kentucky Lake with other adoptive moms at a day retreat I helped organized. I helped lead discussions and shared our story. This gathering of adoptive moms was evidence adoption is relational to its core and another reminder that God hears our desires. I had prayed years ago God would use our story, and here I was with a front-row seat watching Him do that. I left that retreat with new friends, inspiration to continue holding fast to what I knew to be true, and hope God had more chapters to write in our story.

While these women shared about adopting from China, Liberia, Ethiopia, and Haiti, I felt God opening my heart to a third adoption that may not look like our others. My kids were almost eight and six years old. The idea of adopting a child who wasn't a newborn seemed like an option for our family for the first time.

A few days after the retreat, Greg and I found ourselves alone in the minivan. I can't remember how that happened or where we were going, but I seized the moment.

"What do you think about international adoption?" I spoke those words even though we had agreed to stop pursuing adoption a year and a half earlier. The words seemed risky – not with Greg, but to speak aloud.

Greg admitted he too had been thinking about adopting again. God united us when we knew it was time to lay it down, and here He was keeping us in sync as we considered picking up the desire again.

Of course, being the Type-A planner I am, I started researching which countries would be a good fit for us. A Kentucky adoption agency we had heard good things about had a couple international adoption programs that interested us. Greg had a relationship with this agency from some legal work had done for clients. He sent an email to the director, requesting more information on the Korea and Hong Kong programs and asking some general questions.

Then God kept showing up in ways, reminding me He never stopped working.

In the week after Greg and I revived adoption conversations, Ben was recovering from a tonsillectomy. While I was laying low with him, three unrelated friends separately asked if we were still interested in adopting and then referenced specific situations. We said yes, yes, yes. Of course we were interested.

We were interested in finding out more about the woman in Indiana who wanted to connect with a family to adopt the baby she was carrying. Our mutual friend advised me to send her some information about us, so I did via email. But by the time I did, she had already found a family. I found myself thankful for this woman choosing life and excited for the couple who would become parents. Those weren't the emotions I expected, but, again, I was experiencing peace.

A second friend casually mentioned he may know someone interested in talking about adoption. He didn't know many details, but we went with our usual "Of course, we'd love to talk to her about adoption."

Initially, we most intrigued by what was the third scenario – a Kenyan baby girl who a missionary found in a bush. We have a dear friend from Kenya and immediately started a conversation with him about this. Turns out, international adoption from Kenya is nearly impossible. Our friend Daniel and his connections there offered some advice I passed along to the lady who was the go-between the missionary and me.

As I was drafting the email to this lady on May 5, 2015, my phone rang with a familiar number. Turns out, that second friend had more details and wanted us to talk about adoption with Stacy – right then. So he connected her to me via a three-way phone call as I hit send on the email that closed the door to the Kenyan baby I wanted to rescue.

Stacy and I talked about private adoption in general, my family's previous experiences specifically, her motivation for making an adoption plan, and our families. When I asked her where she wanted to go from here, she surprised me with her answer: "I have an ultrasound appointment next week if you want to come."

Yes, of course I want to come.

And I wanted to shout from the rooftops how I was witnessing God working. I called Greg to tell him about the phone call. Basically the conversation went like this: Hey, husband, turns out I met the birth mom for our third child. I later learned Greg and the guys in his Bible study had prayed that morning we would have clarity regarding possibly adopting again.

The adoption agency Greg had contacted a couple weeks earlier had never replied to him, which, really, seemed odd. We learned his contact had left that agency for a different job. Well, the same day I connected with Stacy, someone else from the agency emailed Greg. She apologized his email was overlooked. He told her we didn't need the information on Hong Kong and Korea, but we did need domestic adoption home study information.

Talk about clarity.

I had begun the conversation with Stacy sharing about why we loved private adoption and hoping to help this woman who wanted a plan. By the end of a single twenty-minute phone call, God surprised me with a birth mom for our third child – and she lived less than a mile from us.

Stacy was twenty-two years old and had two children two and younger with her boyfriend, who was also the birth father of this baby. They had a dramatic relationship, little money, a small support system, and on-and-off-again jobs – all variables in her choosing adoption.

Almost two years later, Stacy reflected on our initial conversation and the relief our connection brought her:

> "I wanted her to have a better life than I knew I could provide. When I first talked to you on the phone, I felt God bought us together for a reason and I was already feeling a sense of relief when we got off the phone. When I first met you and Greg, I knew I had found the perfect family and I knew everything was going to be okay."

I didn't shout my excitement from the rooftops or in a Facebook status update, but, thankfully, I did have a birthday dinner planned for that evening with my best friends. We went to a Mexican restaurant, not thinking about Cinco de Mayo being two days after I turned thirty-six, but the busyness didn't bother us because we had plenty to talk about once we got to a table.

Greg and I met Stacy for face-to-face conversation later that same week. She had a sweet spirit and spoke of her relief to have a plan for this child. The following week, we met Stacy and the birth dad at our attorney's office. The four of us talked in the waiting room before our attorney shared with the birth parents what the legal process will look like. This attorney is our friend and has pictures of Ben's adoption finalization on his book shelf because he is the one who connected us with Ben's birth mom in 2009 after finalizing Cate's adoption in 2007.

At twenty-one weeks along, Stacy invited us – again, officially – to her doctor's appointment that included an ultrasound on May 21, 2015. Sure, I was excited to get a glimpse of our baby and hear about her health, but I was still in awe God was orchestrating a third private adoption for us and giving us a second opportunity to love on a local birth mom. During the ultrasound, the baby girl wasn't fully cooperating with her position, but everything was good and we got another look a few weeks later.

We got the best look a few minutes after 1 o'clock in the afternoon on Saturday, September 19, 2015, when we held a swaddled, fresh-from-the-womb Rachel Elizabeth Taylor.

———

Between May and September 2015, Greg and I got to know Stacy. We may have been neighbors in a small town, but we lived in completely different worlds. Having been through two other private adoptions, I wasn't expecting the third time to be such an eye-opening journey.

We hadn't known each other long, but Greg and I had been to two ultrasound appointments and the attorney's office together and I'd taken her to another appointment and the pharmacy. On one particular afternoon, as we returned from her meeting with the social worker, she told me how Greg and I are generous.

Yet she was the one carrying the life of our daughter.

We sat there outside her apartment and talked about this adoption. She was twenty-six weeks pregnant and relieved to have a plan. We talked about post-partum counseling and resources to help her mother well the two children she already had.

"You all are so generous to me," she said. I still think about her words.

I wasn't new to adoption, but Stacy's simple comment shed new light on my relationship with her as a birth mom. I thought about Mandy and Leigh. They were each in different places in life and our connections were each unique. But open adoption was good for my momma soul and I believe it was good for them, too.

That's the beauty of adoption. It's relational in the truest sense.

When Stacy was thirty-one weeks pregnant, I took her to another doctor appointment. As we sat in the waiting room together that afternoon, we talked about how the hospital part of the process may go.

"You can hold the baby first. That first moment is important for a mom and baby," Stacy said. "I can hold her second."

She volunteered to go second because she put Rachel first. That's what generosity and bravery look like.

Yes, we helped her. We made an adoption plan for this child for whom she didn't believe she could care given her circumstances. We covered medical and legal expenses and we put some minutes on her cell phone. I picked her up for appointments.

In terms of money, that's not really very much, even though I know Stacy wasn't measuring our generosity in dollars and cents.

For us, we've believed for years we were supposed to be a family of five. We're ready to expand our family and Stacy made that possible. Talk about generosity.

———

Greg and I were wearing matching Team Taylor T-shirts the day Rachel was born. And we didn't even plan it.

Well, we planned to wear the Team Taylor shirts because we were going to be part of some Hazel Day festivities and they advertised Greg's business. Cate and Ben were even wearing theirs too because if there is ever a time for a family to match it's at a small-town festival.

At first I thought it was a dorky coincidence. But then I saw the beauty in the detail: Team Taylor. We're so grateful our team grew by one that day.

After having an ultrasound and being monitored for a while the previous day, Stacy and the doctor made a plan for her to be induced early the coming Wednesday morning. Although she had been sick that morning with a stomach bug, Stacy was disappointed she was sent home Friday after talk of a possible induction because she was ready.

Apparently Rachel was ready, too.

Stacy called me Saturday morning at 7:59 a.m. to tell me she was having regular contractions and needed to go to the hospital. Our family of four had just pulled into his office driveway in Hazel, a little town just south of Murray. Our family, along with other Taylors, was going to be the grand marshals in the parade and then host an activity at his new second office.

That's what the other Taylors did while we hung out at the hospital in matching shirts. We greeted our daughter just after she was born at 1:09 p.m. She was seven pounds, three ounces and nineteen inches.

It's natural to compare adoption processes, even though, like each child, we recognize they're naturally different. We've brought home three babies as newborns – two from our local hospital. Each time God showed me something new, but He never neglected to show up in the details.

My favorite nurse from Ben's birth in 2009 was there. She took my all-time favorite hospital photo then and almost six years later remembered our story. We chatted throughout the day. She celebrated adoption while being sensitive to the delicate balance of grief and joy happening in one delivery room.

Stacy is a private person so instead of being right by her bedside when Rachel was born, we were just outside the delivery room door. We could hear the last moments of delivery, when our girl entered the world. The birth dad stepped out to hug us and then we were invited in to meet Rachel. I touched her and photographed her while the pediatrician examined her and the nurse weighed her.

Then that favorite delivery nurse of mine handed me Rachel wrapped like a burrito, and I handed her my iPhone with the camera ready to go. She snapped pictures of Greg and me meeting Rachel. She kept snapping pictures as I handed Rachel to Stacy, who graciously went second just like she promised, and then as the four of us gathered around a baby girl we all loved.

We ended up spending about 90 minutes with Stacy after Rachel's birth. We took turns holding her and chatted about our other kids – my two who were eager to meet their baby sister and her two who weren't yet two and three years old.

These moments were open adoption at its finest.

Greg, Rachel and I visited with Stacy later that evening as she recovered in another room and then again the next day when we met with our attorney and social worker before we went our separate ways with all our mixed emotions.

Even in her grief, Stacy knew adoption was the right plan for her – and Rachel. She elaborated on that about eighteen months after the delivery:

> "I feel like I did a good thing. Not only did you guys help me out, but I also helped you in this blessing. I'm grateful to have given birth to another beautiful and perfect baby. Adoption is not selfish. It's one of the most unselfish things you can do. If you truly know the baby would be better off with a different family, then you are thinking of others, not yourself. It's also a beautiful way to create everlasting bonds and I'm so grateful that this was God's plan. It's a blessing to have Rachel in such a good home. I couldn't have asked for a better family."

I stayed at the hospital with Rachel that first night and then, thankfully, she was discharged at twenty-five hours old. Although the kids had met her at the hospital, coming home and having my family of five under the same roof was exactly where I wanted to be – dorky matching shirts included.

I know open adoption seems scary and awkward, but when it's the situation God designed the ways of this world don't apply. Stacy and I may have gone to different homes that Sunday afternoon, but our lives are forever intertwined. Pictures and visits followed, the future was uncertain as it is in these kind of relationships, but Stacy will forever be part of our family's story.

Adoption is a funny process. You spend all this time waiting and then gathering paperwork and then usually waiting some more. There are road blocks and emotions and timelines that don't always matter. And then you bring a child into your home, go about everyday life, and then months later, the adoption is actually finalized.

On December 10, 2015, Rachel's adoption finalization hearing was less than ten minutes long and that involved a quick photo shoot with the judge and attorney. That's a quick end to what has been a much longer process.

Technically, we wanted to adopt a third time since the beginning of 2012. And here we were at the end of 2015. That's basically four years. And we couldn't make it work any quicker.

Of course we couldn't. Rachel Elizabeth was meant to be part of our family and this was our time. Thanks be to God for this season and His faithfulness to do a new thing.

When I look into Rachel's brown eyes and see her joy-filled smile, I remember I was silly for trying to rush into this.

———

One Sunday when Rachel was just a couple weeks old, we sang "Oceans" during worship. I'd never really attached to the song like so many other Christians I know did. But that morning, the song fell on me fresh.

> "Spirit lead me where my trust is without borders / Let me walk upon the waters / Wherever You would call me / Take me deeper than my feet could ever wander / And my faith will be made stronger / In the presence of my Savior"[10]

I couldn't get the phrase "trust without borders" out of my head. I love when God does that. I love knowing He can take words I've heard hundreds of times before and make them sound brand new.

Trust without borders.

That's what I want – in all areas of my life. But I had been thinking about my relationship with Stacy. I was no stranger to open adoption, but the post-birth interaction with Stacy was different than our other experiences. My emotions about the grief intertwined with joy in adoption spill over more easily now.

---

[10] Hillsong UNITED. Oceans (Where Feet My Fail). Hillsong Music Publishing, 2012.

In those weeks right after Rachel's birth, I wanted to mother my baby's birth mom after she confided in me via text and trusted me the details of her life. We got together for the first time since the birth about an hour at a local coffee shop not long before Rachel's first Thanksgiving.

In those days while we were waiting to finalize Rachel's adoption, Stacy and her boyfriend were having trouble. Emotions and drug use compounded already dire circumstances. Without going into details of various situations, for their privacy and because I don't know the whole story, the boyfriend ended up in jail for about a year and Stacy later unexpectedly lost custody of her two kids.

I love these people and I was heartbroken for them. I directed her to counseling and prayed for them all. I wanted to buy her groceries, help her find a job, and encourage her do what she needs to do to regain custody of her two kids. With my third baby in my arms, I didn't know what that meant for my relationship with Stacy.

Stacy told me how those first months after the delivery were hard for reasons related to adoption in addition to all her other circumstances:

> "The first couple of months were very hard and I didn't know how to get past it. I was scared Rachel would feel like I abandoned her, but what helped me was knowing this was part of God's plan and He brought all of us together for a reason. I missed her, but I knew it was the best option for everyone and that's what was most important."

We were brought together, and I wanted to be there for her. Prayers may not seem tangible, but they're gifts. Giving her money or groceries or ride somewhere is easy compared to navigating an actual relationship. I'm open to having a relationship with her even though I have absolutely no idea what that will look like. I'm guessing it's always going to look different from season to season and from any other relationship I have.

I believe this is where God is calling me, so I need to go there. And I can only go there with God. My human self wants a plan and details for the future. But when I trust the One who orchestrated this relationship, my faith becomes stronger and deeper – and going into the unknown becomes possible.

I'm the kind of girl who wants every relationship I've ever had to remain. I want to be friends forever with everyone. As I'm growing up, I realize that isn't how every relationship should be. Adoption magnifies that with its unique relationships, but it also opens the door to a ministry of being able to help someone in a way not otherwise possible.

This may have been our third adoption, but I saw this generosity in adoption in a new light. I thought about Mandy and Leigh, again. Like with Stacy, I've bonded quickly with these women I wouldn't otherwise know. That's what happens when everyone is invested in the same growing life and gathers in exam rooms. We've gotten to know each other in ways that make me proud to tell our children about their beginnings and given these women peace about their plans for adoption.

Then after the birth, the relationships change – at least that's been our experiences. Our adoptions are open in the sense that the birth moms know our names and have our contact information. I send updates about the kids and I'm Facebook friends with two of them. But after the babies were born and final papers signed, we all settled back into our lives. The conversations between us are fewer now and we don't make plans to show up at appointments together anymore.

Stacy wanted monthly visits after Rachel was born, which was fine with me. In Rachel's first year, we saw each other five times and then again when Rachel was about eighteen months old.

In a booth at Subway, I watched them together when Rachel was eighteen months old. I saw a beautiful, striking physical resemblance as Rachel shared Stacy's Doritos. Their circumstances and life situations are vastly different, but their eyes, nose, and smile are the same. Even though people are always amazed at how my family physically fits together, I'm grateful to see evidence of their connection, regardless of what happens with our relationship as Rachel grows up.

My continued relationship with Stacy brings to mind Psalm 68:6 says, "God places the lonely in families ..." and realize how true that is. Yes, God has placed our three children who needed families in our family. But he also put these birth moms in our lives. They may not do everyday life with us, but they're prayed for regularly and remembered gratefully.

Because of adoption they have someone else on their side in life.

Obviously, all adoptions are different. Another family's story may not look like ours, but they all involve generosity. For as similar as our kids' adoption stories are, the relationships we have with their birth moms are the biggest difference.

Cate has met hers and will likely see her again in coming years. Rachel has been held by hers more than either of my other two, but at this point that's not something she will remember. Then in the middle is my tender-hearted boy. He doesn't ask questions about adoption like his big sister does – and maybe that is God protecting Ben's heart. While I have a relationship with his birth mom Leigh, he doesn't at this point.

With anything, the future is unknown, and adoption is no exception. We have open relationships with all three birth moms, but what those relationships look like now vary and that's likely to be the case down the road. These are the kinds of differences that are hard to explain because there are no black-and-white answers regarding human emotions.

But one answer remains true: God chose these three to be in our family. He chose Greg and me to parent them on this earth. And He has adopted us all into His kingdom – which is far greater than anything we can cling to on this earth.

As we sang "Oceans" and I held my third-born baby, I realized I too often try to tie my faith up in a box with a pretty bow. My relationship with Stacy is just one example. I've been there, hesitating, in a million other ways in marriage, motherhood, my daily life, our mission trip to Guatemala, and so many moments between.

Faith isn't always tidy. Sometimes it spills all over the place, bringing us to God in a new way. Our faith takes us places that are messy, but God goes with us, bringing beauty from those ashes.

And sometimes He makes that happen by connecting neighbors.

In Their Words :: Mary Jost

I have two children who were both adopted as babies, but their adoptions and stories are so very different.

My daughter was placed with us when she was two days old after we went through an adoption consultant and agency. Her birth mom placed her in my arms at the hospital before she left. I was fortunate enough to meet both of her birth parents and talk with them. In the ten minutes I spent with them in the hospital room, I learned more about their personalities and their hilarious sense of humor. They also told me why they chose my husband and me to be our daughter's parents. I will cherish that conversation for as long as I live. We have seen my daughter's birth parents a few times in her first almost five years of life and are open to future visits as well. Her birth mom and I occasionally text and speak on the phone, and I mail them letter updates and pictures.

My son came to us when he was two months and two days old when an investigator with the Department of Family and Child Services brought him to my house. I won't ever forget opening the door and laying eyes on him for the first time. It took us thirteen months to finalize his adoption. His case was not the norm for foster care. He never had a single visit with either of his biological parents while he was in foster care. We know plenty of information about his biological family that I will share little by little with him in an age-appropriate way. We do not visit with his biological family nor do we have any form of contact with them – and there are no plans for us to in the future.

My daughter has noticed there is a difference in her adoption and her brother's and my son may when he's older. She has asked questions about why we don't keep in touch or visit with his biological family but we do with hers. At first it was tricky navigating the questions from a young child. I don't want to lie or hide the truth in any way from my kids. Their stories are beautiful even though they come from a place of brokenness. God sure does make beauty from ashes!

I have found ways to tell my daughter the difference in their adoption stories and biological families and still be age appropriate while not hiding the truth. For now, I have stopped worrying about the differences in their stories and choose to rejoice while thanking God for the differences. Their stories are proof of God's love and power and grace – and that's a story worth sharing.

Mary Jost is a proud wife and mom who tries her best to raise Jesus-loving kids in the South.

In Their Words :: Melody Hester

From the time our kids were babies we would recount the day we brought them home from the adoption agency. Complete with detail that included sounds – sound of the phone ringing when we "got the call" and unfortunately even the sound of the police siren pulling us over because we were so excited to get our new baby home that we were speeding. Ooops!

For months and years after we would tell the story the same way and the kids picked up on all the parts of the story so that it soon became their story to tell.

As our children got older the story stayed the same and wasn't shared as often but harder questions came up along the way. Sometimes it would be in the middle of our son building Legos on the floor. He'd say, "Why would anybody give up their baby?" Other times out of the blue he would point to a random woman and say, "Could that be the lady whose tummy I grew in?"

They don't ask these questions in the middle of reading a book on adoption. It's always when you least expect it and out of nowhere. But it should tell us that these are thoughts going through their minds even when they're not saying it. So for it to come out in the open is a beautiful thing. Embrace it and don't be afraid to talk about it.

Innate feelings of rejection and abandonment are natural for anyone and especially that of an adopted child. And no matter how positive you are about the birth parents situation (and we are very positive focusing on the loving decision she made to place through adoption) and no matter how quickly you bonded and are loving toward your children, they may feel a deep sense of abandonment that they might not even be able to express in words.

The ages of six to twelve are important years in developing identity. In these years you might have difficult but good conversations. Life Science class will ask your child to write down their recessive and dominant genes.

They might be the only one in class with a blank paper. That's hard. But redeem this difficult moment for a better understanding of our true identity being in Christ alone, not our genetic makeup. We are image bearers of Jesus Christ. Before they were born God knew what they would look like and where they would call home and who they'd call Mom and Dad. That's just awesome!

Oh, and what about the people in the Bible who were adopted? We talk about them a lot, too. Moses and, of course, Jesus – we forget about that sometimes, don't we?

I now look back on some of the hard conversations with our children and I'm thankful we chose to talk through them. Even the times we had no answer, and the pain and wounds were raw. Prayer covers you through those times.

Once your child is adopted into Christ's family that also is a beautiful thing. Our son said, "Hey, I've been adopted twice now!" when he became a Christian. Over time I saw a confidence build inside of him. As his faith grew in Christ so did the assurance of his identity as a believer and as a part of our family. And isn't that what we desire most? For our kids to walk closely with Jesus on this earth as His adopted children.

Melody Hester is a stumbling Christ follower, wife, and mom. The process of infertility, miscarriage, and adoption were painfully beautiful crucibles that brought her closer to Jesus. She blogs about life at www.lifeisabowlofwedgies.com.

How God Surprises Us

See, I am doing a new thing! Now it springs up; do you not perceive it?
I am making a way in the wilderness and streams in the wasteland.

(Isaiah 43:19)

I wanted my three kids close in age. But, not surprisingly, God's timing was better, perfect even.

We welcomed Rachel when Cate was eight and Ben was two months from turning six. And, let me tell you, they have adored their baby sister from the beginning. They literally argued over who is going to hold her or sit next to her in the van. For many months, we maintained a week-to-week rotation of who is in the middle of the minivan next to Rachel and who had to settle for the very back seat.

Cate was a feeding champion – although I never could convince her she could be a master diaper changer, too! Since Rachel was a day old, Ben has wanted to be near her, even venturing downstairs into her room a few times in the middle of the night when he heard her crying for her next bottle. This boy was meant to be a middle child. With the initials BLT, he's perfectly sandwiched between two girls.

And it's clear Rachel wants to keep up with the big kids – and I'm assuming that will always be the case.

For this momma of three, having two in school and a baby at home was a whole different world than last time I had a baby – and a toddler. Beyond logistics, God prepared me to be a mom again. My perspective was different and I'm more confident. I brought more than eight years of motherhood experiences with me this time.

I have a theory about third-born girls being feisty and funny. I can name several third-born girls — my sister, nieces, and friends' daughters quickly come to mind — who are so much fun to be around. They're the kind of people who have confidence that keeps them from being wallflowers, a joy that lights up a room, and a sense of humor that makes even adults chuckle.

Honestly, I always wanted a third-born girl, so being able to adopt a third child who was a girl was especially exciting for me. She's proven my theory true in the best ways.

She's proving the whole idea that rules don't apply to third-born kids true, too … but perhaps that's because Greg and I are a little more laid-back in our parenting this time around. And speaking of birth order, here's a fun fact: All three of my kids' birth order is the same in our family as it would have been in their biological families. Only God.

I quickly learned why third babies were spoiled. And I mean that in a completely endearing way. This third baby brought so much joy to our family and to so many other people. I'm Facebook friends with one of the local Post Office workers because Rachel has charmed herself behind the counter for suckers so many times.

Before Rachel was born, I was ready — not ready like my house was perfect and my life completely under control, but ready in that my heart knew what God had done and I was willing to embrace what He was going to do. I was in place I could truly rejoice in His faithfulness. In 2014 and 2015, God taught me much about joy. And then He surprised me with Rachel, who embodies joy to the fullest.

I'm grateful to be a mom of three for many reasons, but especially because I believe this is what God planned for me. Yes, I had doubts this third time would happen, and I was going to be okay with that because my life already overflowed with blessings. But I'm grateful I indeed heard God right years ago about the third child, even if my timing was totally out of sync with God's.

———

Each month during her first year, I documented Rachel's life with posts on my blog about what she was into and what milestones she reached. She was nine months old on Father's Day 2016, so I invited Greg to share on my blog that day:

"Every year when Father's Day rolls around, I am reminded that our God is faithful. It's a time for me to look back and reflect on His goodness and grace in my life. I am so undeserving, and yet He has blessed me with three small souls to love and lead.

In looking back, I can tell you He uses my children to change me daily. The Holy Spirit convicts me of my own shortcomings through the questions and conversations had with my two older inquisitive children. As we live life with them, I hope that they can hear and see the reality of God's grace through my attitudes and actions.

My own father passed away in 2010, and I can tell you that I learned how to follow God by watching him. He followed God with his whole heart and was the example for me and my brothers on how to lead our families.

Hopefully, Kristin and I have learned a few things about parenting in these more than nine years. Mostly, I think we've learned the children need to see Kristin and me mess up, and see what it means to ask for and receive forgiveness from each other and God.

This year, in reflecting on Father's Day, it is amazing to think about how last April, we had no idea that Rachel was even on the horizon. We had felt the Lord calling us to adopt again in 2012 and looked into several options, but never had the right situation.

Kristin and I were disappointed and frustrated, but eventually we just realized that we had already been amazingly blessed by the Lord to have our two children. And so we mostly gave up our hope of adopting a third child. Our hearts were still pulled toward adopting a third child, but we finally had the grateful perspective that we needed. We learned a bit about being content in any situation and then, when we least expected it, we got a phone call from Rachel's birth mom.

Rachel has been such an amazingly sweet addition to our family. Ben and Cate were immediately taken with their new sister, and she has responded in kind. Rachel has an engaging smile that she flashes to almost everyone.

And the best part is that Rachel has two older siblings to look up to and learn from. I love watching her interact with them every day. So on this Father's Day, I am going to reflect on the goodness of our Heavenly Father and rejoice in His provision in my life. I pray you can do the same."

———————

Here I was a mom of three kids, and one word rocked my world. One word shifted my perspective.

Ambassador.

It jumped out at me when I was working through a Sermon on the Mount study the fall my kids were nine, seven, and one. I was reading about being peacemakers when the study took us to some verses from Second Corinthians. Of course, my mind went to parenting.

"Therefore, if anyone is in Christ, the new creation has come: The old has gone, the new is here! All this is from God, who reconciled us to himself through Christ and gave us the ministry of reconciliation: that God was reconciling the world to himself in Christ, not counting people's sins against them. And he has committed to us the message of reconciliation. We are therefore Christ's ambassadors, as though God were making his appeal through us. We implore you on Christ's behalf: Be reconciled to

God. God made him who had no sin to be sin for us, so that in him we might become the righteousness of God" (2 Corinthians 5:17-21).

I was dwelling on the fact I'm a representative of Christ to my children as I went about life one day in the fall of 2016, which happened to be a hard one. Disappointments and inconveniences filled that day.

While waiting for my kids at the bus stop that October day, I finally opened *Parenting: 14 Gospel Principles That Can Radically Change Your Family* by Paul David Tripp because I had said I would read and review it on my blog. The deadline was approaching and I needed to get started. If I'm honest, I procrastinated reading it because the subtitle sounded just like something I needed. And change is hard.

AMBASSADOR. It was the first word in the whole book, the title of the introduction. Four pages in, and I was crying. I was grieving and dealing with conviction and rejoicing with hope.

I couldn't even finish the introduction in that sitting because I had to digest this more: My kids don't belong to me, but I'm Christ's ambassador to them. I know, it's probably not even a new concept to most Christ-followers, but it was striking me in a fresh way I still can't shake.

Because of my emotions and revelations, I needed a couple days to get through the introduction of Paul David Tripp's book, but the shift in perspective was exactly what I've needed to be a better wife and mom.

Tripp starts the book writing about the differences between ownership and ambassadorial parenting. Basically, our human default is to treat our families as possessions. It doesn't seem bad because we talk about the good things we want for and from our children. We talk about goals and hopes and dreams we have for these people we love. But we get really caught up in producing those things by ourselves.

We leave out the One who truly creates families. Ambassadors faithfully represent the message, methods, and character of another leader – in our case, Jesus.

I've always given credit to God for creating our family, but thinking about how I don't own my family and need to be a representative of Christ to them rocked my world.. In *Parenting*, Paul David Tripp reminded me what was important and truly everlasting:

"Parenting is not first about what we want for our children or from our children, but about what God in grace has planned to do through us in our children."[11]

In a matter of days, this concept made my life harder and easier in the same moment. It gave me focus and convicted my heart. It slowed me down and helped me see beyond the daily frustrations of dirty floors and a never-ending to do list.

And, admittedly, the weight of being an ambassador interrupted my finishing Tripp's book. I eventually read more chapters, but I keep coming back to that introduction about how I'm an ambassador of Christ to my kids.

---

[11] Tripp, Paul David. Parenting: 14 Gospel Principles That Can Radically Change Your Family. Crossway, 2016.

In Their Words :: Katie Cunningham

My husband and I have been in church ministry for 11 years. In that time, adoption is something I have seen become a passion for most in our church body. This has not just been seen in the physical adoptions that have taken place, but also through awareness and monetary support for adoption.

Within my church, five adopted girls are in my young daughter's nursery class. Two close friends of mine have teenage foster children. Our church also has helped to build a home for a missionary family who needed more room because it was growing through adoption. It has become so normal and natural that I don't even think about it anymore. They are not adopted children or foster children; they are just children – sons and daughters of some of my best friends.

Christians, through their local churches, should be liaisons for adoption and orphans because as believers we have been adopted into the family of God. As believers, we should want to replicate that picture of our adoption into God's family. When we adopt children into our families and church bodies as well as support others who do, we are representing the gospel in a powerful way that allows us to point others to the adoption we have in Christ.

Katie Cunningham is a pastor's wife who works in her home raising three sons and a daughter.

How God Heals Through Community

Is anyone among you in trouble? Let them pray. Is anyone happy? Let them sing songs of praise. Is anyone among you sick? Let them call the elders of the church to pray over them and anoint them with oil in the name of the Lord. And the prayer offered in faith will make the sick person well; the Lord will raise them up. If they have sinned, they will be forgiven. Therefore confess your sins to each other and pray for each other so that you may be healed. The prayer of a righteous person is powerful and effective.

(James 5:13-16)

I never expected to adopt, but God prepared us and surrounded us with people who have embraced our journey with us. We are involved with a small, non-denominational church with about 75 people in the sanctuary on Sunday mornings. But in those chairs are families with kids adopted from Nepal, China, and Liberia. Our church also has an orphan/adoption ministry that offers grants and fund-raising support for families pursuing an adoption as well as opportunities to give to local and international projects that support orphans and underserved kids.

Jesus tells us to serve these populations (James 1:27), and I'm blessed with a community that believes in doing and serving and giving and adopting and loving. Not everyone is called to adopt, but God gives us – even in a small town – plenty of opportunities to make a difference.

Since February 2007, we've gathered with our best friends Jaclyn and Bryan on a regular basis to eat dinner and play Settlers of Catan, our favorite board game. Before that, we got to together on Thursdays for dinner and "Survivor," "CSI," and "Grey's Anatomy." Kids made watching

TV together difficult, but our kids haven't stopped the Settlers tradition, which began when there was just one child among us.

Now we have six kids – and the first five were born in five years. That fact alone makes my heart full, after Jaclyn and I walked through hard seasons of infertility together.

The first five kids – born in April 2006, May 2007, April 2008, November 2009, and August 2010 – have prompted us to play Settlers at different times of the day and perfect our multitasking. And, yes, my heart melted when Cate was old enough to play Catan Junior. Now they've got the baby of the bunch to entertain – and, trust me, they like that job, so much so that sometimes they argue about who is in charge.

Perhaps it's a board game addiction, but it's also about community.

These kids don't know life without each other. They celebrate birthdays with each other, build things from Legos, have their own favorite shows, and spend many summer days in the pool together. They're often loud and crazy, but they're the sweetest reminders that God has a plan grander than anything we can construct ourselves.

Our two families are part of a bigger community we cherish, too.

The same year Ben was born our small group from church started a tradition. I'm not sure we knew it was going to be a tradition, but this group – equal parts kids and adults – gathered around a table for a Thanksgiving meal.

That was 2009. And, actually, Greg and I didn't get to go because Ben was born on that Monday afternoon. We brought him home Tuesday afternoon, just hours before they had our first Thanksgiving. Not only did we not go, but my friend Sarah – who had a boy just shy of a month old – made the green bean casserole I was supposed to bring. And then our friends brought us plates overflowing with delicious food. We weren't at the actual table with them that first year, but we were with them and they were with us.

Community works that way.

Four years later, we were still gathering around the table for a Thanksgiving meal, and it was when I broke out my china plates for the first time. For more than eleven years, that china has been sitting around, supposedly waiting for a "special occasion." Truth be told, I was persuaded to register for the china and really wouldn't regret had I not added it. But I have it. And I decided having it sit there was pointless.

Really, everyday community is a special occasion.

We're not technically in an official small group with these people because we scattered to build relationships with other generations in our church, but these people are our community. Together, we've mourned and prayed and dreamed and hoped and planned and played and cheered and cried and laughed.

My girlfriends even washed, by hand, the china plates I probably would have put in the dishwasher. They're into the ordinary details like that. They're helpful like that. We're in this life together like that.

In 2013, I snapped a picture of the nine kids who ranged in age from seven months to seven years and were gathered for the Fifth Annual Thanksgiving with Friends. I noticed Ben being part of the group in his school uniform, little blue shirt. He was a day old when this group first gathered around a table, literally, to give thanks for how we gather around the table, figuratively, with each other in our daily lives. He's grown up knowing those other kids who surround him on the couch and their parents. He's grown up in community.

In 2016, the kid contingent had grown to eleven for our Eighth Annual Thanksgiving with Friends. I still didn't have a clever name for the gathering, but we still had each other, even though one family had moved several hours away. That was the year we traded the china for paper plates – and nobody cared.

God made Greg, Cate, Ben, Rachel, and me a family. But He's expanded our family because we're part of His family.

Truth be told, this community amazes me. God built community around me with these families and others when I wondered if it would happen. I moved back to my college town that is also my husband's hometown when I was twenty-three. I couldn't imagine people my age would move into a rural college town on the edge of far western Kentucky. Jaclyn had stayed after she had her degree in hand, and we were thankful for each other when I moved back.

That would have been plenty, but God did more. He surprised us with community in a town I wasn't sure would be able to offer us new friends. Some friends have moved. Other friendships have changed with the normal rhythm of life. We've made new friends and kept the old. Thankfully, that community continues to happen right here around my table.

———

Greg and I have married friends who work in ministry with international college students in New York City. In the summer of 2016, they were visiting our town because it is also the husband's hometown. This was the same summer we had a baby who learned to get into everything just as we moved to a new-to-us house that involved some renovations. Among the first people to visit our new house, some things these friends shared about their ministry struck a chord with me.

I already knew God called me to share with and serve moms – young moms who don't have much support, adoptive moms, birth moms, women who are surprised by pregnancy and not sure what to do about it, women who want to be moms but are in seasons of infertility and waiting. That's different than the Muslims my friends serve in the nation's biggest city. But what they shared made sense in my small-town heart.

We can ask people to come – into our churches, into our homes, into our lives, into our ways of doing things – but doing so isn't going to prompt their first steps. Instead, we should be willing to go to them. We need to step into their lives and stories with no strings attached. We need to love them wherever they are.

We need to stop saying "come ..." and be willing to go.

I knew that night, sitting in my not-yet-decorated living room with out-of-town friends, where I needed to go. Apparently going to Guatemala a year earlier was just part of the story. This time going wasn't going to be as many miles away.

For years, Greg and I have supported the crisis pregnancy center in Murray. We gave Life House Care Center our crib when I couldn't stand to wonder if we'd actually ever need it again. We've donated diapers and dollars throughout the years and participated in fundraising events they hosted. Greg even serves on the board.

I had talked to Life House's director, Stephanie, about volunteering there … one day, you know, when all my kids were in school and I was looking for a new thing. But that night after our friends shared what God was doing in New York, I knew God was doing something here, too. I sent Stephanie a Facebook message that explained how I believed God was leading me to volunteer there sooner than "one day."

She asked if I could start the training so I could meet with clients who come into Life House. I ended up reading a training manual and then talking about it with Stephanie and Hailey, who works there and was the client services director. I shadowed Hailey and asked a ton of questions, befriending her along the way. After several weeks, I started meeting with clients, most of whom came to Life House for its earn-while-you-learn program that allows them to acquire life skills while earning pretend money to shop with for baby clothes, diapers, and other supplies.

Not long after I started volunteering for three hours each Wednesday morning, a college girl whose story reminded me of Mandy's from nearly a decade earlier sat in the counseling room weighing her options, which she had narrowed to abortion or adoption. I told her our story. I told her about Mandy. I told her about Cate, and a little about Ben and Rachel, too.

In that conversation and others that have followed with women in different situations, I realized God prepared me to be there. The years of waiting and wondering, the navigating relationships with three birth moms, and the mothering small children had prepared me to serve women who needed someone on their side.

I was heartbroken when Hailey told me that college girl who reminded me of my own daughter's birth mom ended up choosing abortion at sixteen weeks pregnant. Many months later, I still think about her. I pray she meets Jesus and realizes her decision – the one that was influenced by fear of what her parents would think, desire to please her boyfriend who didn't even go to the two-day abortion appointment with her, and darkness that exists right here in our broken world – doesn't have to define her.

————

On our fourteenth anniversary, Greg and I sat in a busy breakfast cafe on Hilton Head Island, taking advantage of extra adult hands to take care of our kids at the beach house our party of sixteen was occupying for the week. We ended up talking about how God has opened our eyes through adoption to the hurting moms in our small town and how He then provided the opportunity for me to volunteer at Life House. I struggled to articulate some thoughts and got frustrated, so much so I declared we needed to talk about something else. We talked about another less meaningful topic momentarily, but then we ended back on the harder stuff.

I was grasping how adoption had changed me from the inside out. I knew God used adoption to build my faith while He was building my family, but I had a new perspective of what my story could do for others. Just as God was working out this new chapter in my heart and I had some time to talk about it with Greg, I read *Falling Free: Rescued from the Life I Always Wanted* by Shannan Martin, whose family has their own stories of adoption and faith.

Like our friends in New York, our callings aren't the same, but Shannan affirmed some of what God has been telling me. Her story reminded me that God does want to make broken things and people beautiful – and He uses those pieces of life we least expected to do it.

"Though we didn't realize it then, adoption was our earliest entry point away from the comfort of the status quo and through the doorway of tangible distress and loss. It was here that I began to see, for the first time, that perhaps what the world calls 'brokenness' can be a thing of real beauty, adorned in the best possible ways, unexpected and entirely holy."[12]

As Christians, we like to do Bible studies and acquire more and more knowledge, which is fine, but that can't be all we do. (Trust me, I know. I like reading books, too!) We have to go do something with what, especially Who, we know. We have to go and serve and love. Then we can invite them into our churches and into our lives and into our homes – and hopefully they'll want to come.

Greg and I took this idea to the next level as 2017 began and started a new small group focused on local service.

We left the comforts of a small group through our church. These people who spanned different generations have loved our family so well. They prayed for us when we started contemplating a third adoption again. They rejoiced with us when Rachel was born and prayed for us as we navigated other parenting seasons. They welcomed us in their homes and lives. They accepted our invitations, helped us move, and became our friends.

Stepping out in faith to do something new with God didn't mean sacrificing friends but rather taking what they'd taught us and sharing it with others. Even so, leaving that group was bittersweet.

In January 2017, we gathered with what was shaping up to be our new small group in the same living room where God had spoken to my heart through our friends from New York. It's the living room where Rachel took her first steps toward her brother and sister. It's where our family gathers to watch "Fixer Upper." Toys are scattered. Often whatever book Cate is reading can be found on the couch. Ben is notorious for leaving his socks there. It's where life has happened and will continue to happen.

The living room is also where I learned more about peace – specifically the depth of "shalom," a Greek word that has weaved its way into my

---

[12] Martin, Shannan. *Falling Free: Rescued from the Life I Always Wanted.* Nashville: Thomas Nelson, 2016.

American life. Jesus is our Prince of Peace (Isaiah 9:6) and wants to make us complete. "Shalom" literally means completeness, soundness, welfare, peace.[13] Yes, the absence of conflict is good, but really the completeness is what Jesus makes possible.

Adoption has shown me how God brings order to brokenness, but it's also opened my eyes to the community around me. I want to help bring peace – the lasting kind that changes us from the inside out – to people. That's part of what our small group strives to do, for each other and for the people we serve.

In her book *Never Unfriendea*, Lisa-Jo Baker taught me more about peace. Yes, her book is about friendship, but it reached down deeply into my soul and my past experiences and uncovered new layers for me. She introduced me to a new perspective on peace:

> "The kind of shalom we're challenged to give to the people around us requires us to take an active interest in their physical and spiritual well-being. ... In addition to caring deeply about seeing conflict come to an end, shalom is passionately invested in seeking the well-being of others – other people, other places and cultures and neighbors. ... Shalom is a radical word that challenges us to wake up from our obsession with ourselves and instead start the deliberate choice of focusing on the people around us ..."[14]

That first night eleven adults from three churches gathered in my living room while our seven kids played nearby. We listed a whole page of ways we could serve our community. We threw out names and organizations and needs and ideas. We realized there would be plenty for us to do if we wanted to serve our neighbors in Jesus' name.

---

[13] Isaiah 9:6 at BlueLetterBible.org.
[14] Baker, Lisa-Jo. Never Unfriended: The Secret to Finding & Keeping Lasting Friendships. B&H Publishing, 2017.

After everyone left, I washed dirty dishes and remembered what God had done to get us here. He knitted together five individuals to a make a family through adoption. Because of that and so many other people we've known and places we've been, God opened our eyes to how we can share what we know to be true.

God continued doing a new thing around here through that small group. These words about the peace that comes when we think of others before ourselves strikes me deeply because it's the foundation of so many other things.

The ripples of truly caring about the people around us – those who are like us, those who are different from us, and those who we don't even know – are everlasting.

And I'm guessing we'll be changed in the process, too. Because that's how God works. He doesn't waste moments or relationships. He uses it all – for His glory and our good. But we certainly aren't going to get there alone.

———

Somebody told me Greg and I make beautiful babies. Well, actually we don't – at least not biologically. We do know our kids are beautiful and love their birth moms for that and so, so many other reasons.

But it doesn't stop with their outward appearances. Because these women chose life, Greg and I get the opportunity to make these babies into people – beautiful people. God willing, these babies who were all born with dark hair and easy smiles will grow up to be lovely from the inside out.

Adoption always begins with darkness only God can redeem. Adoption is rooted in grief and loss and poverty and brokenness. But God brings light and purpose and fullness and joy to situations only he can make new.

When Rachel was tiny, I read *Looking for Lovely: Collecting the Moments that Matter* by Annie Downs. It has nothing to do with adoption but everything to do with finding God in the midst of pain and sadness and brokenness. One passage struck me deeply:

> "The pain of broken families and broken hearts sometimes is deeper than words can describe. But there is beauty in choosing to feel that pain, in calling hurt what it is, and not pretending everything is okay. Whatever tragedy you have experienced or are currently living through, the most beautiful thing you can do is LIVE. Keep walking, keep weeping, keep eating. Don't ignore the hurt. Don't attempt to avoid it and just move on with your life. Feel it all, and invite people in to feel it with you."[15]

I can't think of anything more lovely.

When I read this, I thought about the adoption group I host on Facebook, where we share resources and prayers and praises. I remembered where I'd been and what God has done with that brokenness. And I offered thanksgiving – yet again – for my kids' birth moms who made brave decisions in the midst of messy circumstances.

That's why holding my sleeping babies in church has always been holy for me. It's so ordinary, yet it's proof God hears the desires of our hearts and calls us for a specific purpose. A sleeping baby who is at home nestled in the crook of my arm is evidence that God brought light to the darkness.

One Sunday when Rachel was seven months old, I held her while she slept and I remembered when coming to church was hard a decade earlier because people kept announcing pregnancies and I was ready to do the same. I remembered how Cate was born on a Sunday, Ben on a Monday, and then Rachel on a Saturday. Announcing their births was nothing short of miraculous. They're all proof God redeems and makes new.

---

[15] Downs, Annie. *Looking for Lovely: Collecting the Moments that Matter.* B&H Publishing Group, 2016.

With a baby in my arms, church was different than it was a decade ago. Cate has claimed Christ has her savior. Ben was still wiggly but learning to read the words on the slides during worship. And Rachel slept. (Although that sleeping-through-church season is short!) They all belong and I have no doubt Greg and I were chosen to be their parents.

I can't think of anything more holy than that.

But, of course, with that baby in my arms, God had more to teach me.

Our speaker in church talked about prayer and how it heals. While Rachel slept in my arms, I looked up "healed" during the sermon and read "to cure, to make whole."[16] In that moment, I was keenly aware of what God has done through prayers to make our family whole.

We think our family is complete. I say "think" because I've learned never say never when it comes to God. But here we are, a party of five that God orchestrated.

There's evidence of God's faithfulness in my kids' eyes – the girls have matching brown and Ben's are blue like Greg's and mine. There's proof that God hears the desires of our hearts when I remember how we got here.

I wasn't sick in the physical sense, but my body didn't function properly for pregnancy and I have been sick in the spiritual sense. Along this journey to and through motherhood, I've been sad and broken and angry and lost. Yet I've also been happy and fulfilled and peaceful and found.

I think of the prayers – the one I cried out to God, the ones my friends said to God in my presence, the ones I probably don't even know about – and realize that's how we made it here. Adoption built my faith and my family, but the prayers along the way healed my soul and made my family whole.

---

[16] James 5:16 at BlueLetterBible.org.

Resources

Books

A Beautiful Exchange: Responding to God's Invitation for More by Megan Nilsen

Adopted for Daily Life: A Devotional for Adopting Moms by Wendy Willard

Adopted for Life: The Priority of Adoption for Christian Families and Churches by Russell Moore

Before You Were Mine: Discovering Your Adopted Child's Lifestory by Susan Tebos and Carissa Woodwyk

Blessed Chaos: A Journey Through Instant Motherhood by Ashley Wells

Bound by Love – The Journey of Lily Nie and Thousands of China's Forsaken Children by Linda Droeger

Bringing Home the Missing Linck by Jennifer Jackson Linck

Falling Free: Rescued from the Life I Always Wanted by Shannan Martin

Fields of the Fatherless: Discover the Joy of Compassionate Living by Tom Davis

Infertility: A Survival Guide for Couples and Those Who Love Them by Cindy Lewis Dake

Love You More: The Divine Surprise of Adopting My Daughter by Jennifer Grant

Message from an Unknown Chinese Mother: Stories of Loss and Love by Xinran

Orphanology: Awakening to Gospel-Centered Adoption and Orphan Care by Tony Merida

The Connected Child by Karyn Purvis

The Lost Daughters of China: Adopted Girls, Their Journey to America, and the Search for a Missing Past by Karin Evans

The Primal Wound: Understanding the Adopted Child by Nancy Newton Verrier

Twenty Things Adopted Kids Wish Their Adoptive Parents Knew by Sherrie Eldridge

Children's Books

A Mother for Choco by Keiko Kasza

Adopted and Loved Forever by Annetta E. Dellinger

Audrey Bunny by Angie Smith

God Found Us You by Lisa Tawn Bergren

In My Heart - A Book of Feelings by Jo Witek

I Wished for You: An Adoption Story by Marianne Richmond

Mommy's Heart Went Pop by Christina Kyllonen

My Adopted Child, There's No One Like You by Dr. Kevin Leman & Kevin Leman II

Tell Me Again About the Night I Was Born by Jamie Lee Curtis

The Bridge That Love Built: Letting God Fill the Gaps in Your Adoption Story by Amara Bratcher and Sallie Dean

The Skin You Live In by Michael Tyler

Wild About You by Judy Sierra

Yes, I'm Adopted! by Sharlie Zinniger

You Were Always in My Heart by Mary Beth and Steven Curtis Chapman

Websites

Adoption at the Movies – www.adoptionlcsw.com

Christian Alliance for Orphans – www.cafo.org

Confessions of an Adoptive Parent – confessionsofanadoptiveparent.com

Empowered to Connect – empoweredtoconnect.org

Hope That Binds – hopethatbinds.com

Jason Johnson's blog – jasonjohnsonblog.com

Lifesong for Orphans – www.lifesongfororphans.org

Show Hope – showhope.org

Acknowledgements & Thanks

Writing is my therapy, but even so, I needed my people to make this book happen.

Greg – I've been writing longer than I've known you, but you've read so many words and listened to even more that didn't get documented. Thank you for understanding I'm an outward processor, believing our story is worth sharing, and spurring me on toward Jesus.

Jaclyn Tompkins – Thank you for living this story and so many others with me. Our friendship started when we were single college girls and journeyed through so many other seasons until we had each had three kids after we weren't sure either of us would have one. I'm grateful our kids don't know life apart from each other because I don't know how to do life without you.

Sarah Goodrich – I don't know how many times you read this book of mine in the moments you stole while those four kids of yours took breaks from bringing you stacks of their favorite books to read. Thank you for sharing my emotions of this story as if they were your own.

Lois Green and the rest of that Sunday night group – A conversation one Sunday night in February 2014 while we looked up scriptures about how God adopts us and chooses us was just the nudge I needed to write this story. You love our family well.

Kim Todd – You probably had no idea how much your understanding of grief and joy coexisting in those delivery rooms in 2009 and 2015 meant to me, but I'm grateful you were there – and that you snapped our very first pictures of Ben and Rachel.

Kim Crouch – Thank you for leading us in Guatemala and letting me cry that first night at dinner. It was a life-changing week for our family. Gaining you as a dear friend was icing on the cake. I'm thrilled we now also share an adoptive momma bond and our third-born girls can be friends.

Stephanie Kelly, Hailey Roach, and Ali Burge – Thank you for welcoming me into Life House and allowing me to come alongside the awesome work y'all are doing, even for just a few hours a week.

Adoption Together – This community began as an idea in my head and has become one of my favorite online places. I love the resources and prayers that are shared there. I love meeting some of you for lunch regularly and swapping real-life stories. I'm grateful for those of you who took the time to contribute pieces of your stories to this book.

Better Together Bloggers – You ladies have encouraged me well in this calling to be a writer that overlaps every other area of life. I'm thankful for our conversations in our Facebook group, through your blogs and social media posts, in our Voxer messages, and at our weekend together.

Writer friends and blog readers – Thank you for encouraging me to tell this story and for reading so many of my words. You all came alongside me with encouragement and inspiration.

About The Author

Kristin Hill Taylor believes in seeking God as the author of every story and loves swapping these stories with friends on porches. She lives in Murray, Kentucky, with her family.

With this family of extroverts, she can often be found hosting a game night, watching sporting events with friends, meeting friends for lunch, or answering her kids' questions about whether anyone is coming over for dinner. Road trips, roller coasters, word games, and TV shows on Netflix are among her favorite activities.

She has a bachelor's in print journalism from Murray State University and worked in various newsrooms before she became a stay-at-home mom. She volunteers and does freelance projects that involve writing, promoting, organizing, and hosting.

Connect with Kristin all over the Internet:

Blog :: kristinhilltaylor.com

Email :: kristinhilltaylor@gmail.com

Facebook :: www.facebook.com/khtwriter

Twitter :: www.twitter.com/kristinhtaylor

Instagram :: www.instagram.com/kristinhtaylor